Common Ground

Common Ground

Janice Marriott   Virginia Pawsey

HarperCollins*Publishers*

National Library of New Zealand Cataloguing-in-Publication Data

Marriott, Janice.
Common ground / written by Janice Marriott and Virginia Pawsey.
ISBN 978-1-86950-680-3
1. Marriott, Janice—Correspondence. 2. Pawsey, Virginia—
Correspondence. 3. Women gardeners—New Zealand—
Correspondence. I. Pawsey, Virginia. II. Title.
635.092—dc 22a

First published 2008
HarperCollins*Publishers (New Zealand) Limited*
P.O. Box 1, Auckland

ISBN: 978 1 86950 680 3

Cover design by Sarah Bull, Anthony Bushelle Graphics
Internal text design and typesetting by IslandBridge

Printed by Griffin Press, Australia, on 79 gsm Bulky White
79gsm Bulky Paperback used by HarperCollinsPublishers is a natural,
recyclable product made from wood grown in a combination of sustainable
plantation and regrowth forests. It also contains up to a 20% portion of
recycled fibre. The manufacturing processes conform to the environmental
regulations in Tasmania, the place of manufacture.

How we came to write this book

In 1998, Virginia Pawsey (*née* Sinclair) organized a reunion of our small class of Seventh Formers from Gisborne Girls' High School. We spent Waitangi Weekend in Gisborne re-acquainting ourselves with classmates we hadn't seen since our last school assembly.

Gillian organized a picnic for us in Eastwoodhills Arboretum. It was hot. We sat around a picnic table and, while the almost-forgotten power of the Gizzy sun beat down, each of us told our life story. Virginia and I had led totally different lives. However, we had also both suffered tragic bereavements. And we both loved our gardens.

Before the weekend was over, we all did what Gisborne girls always did then and still do today — we all went to the beach and threw ourselves in the surf. Then everyone scattered, back to their own worlds. The Wainui tide swirled in and pulled back out, and the sand was wiped clean.

Virginia and I started emailing each other. We've never stopped emailing since. *Common Ground* is a selection of those emails.

A note about Bunsen

Bunsen the dog, often referred to in the emails, died of old age before this book went to print.

He had spent a happy life in the garden, relishing its convenience the way we humans would a large top-opening freezer. He only had to dig down a bit to find stored food. I am still pulling those cannon bones out of the soil today. I put them under the compost bins. It helps with air flow. We try to ignore the fact the bins are getting taller and taller and looking more and more like Baba Yaga's hut.

Bunsen is buried in his own special part of the garden. Six Hills Giant catmint flourishes above him. It might be inappropriate, but it looks beautiful.

Janice

A shared thank you

Thanks, from both of us, for the terrifying tutelage of Miss Duff and Miss Bullen, Principal and Second in Command at Gisborne Girls' High School, and to Miss Bagley, Miss Knaggs, Mr Simpson and Mr Cruttenden, who taught us not only that girls must wear their hats at all times and never ever face outwards from the hockey field to watch Gisborne Boys High boys biking past, but also — how to write.

An acknowledgment is also due, painful as the recollection is, to *The ABC of English Usage*, a book we had to learn by heart.

In memory of Kit
Virginia

In memory of Boyd
Janice

Janice's Introduction

My garden lies between Tinakori Hill and the Wellington motorway in an area of tiny lanes and old cottages. The house sits in the middle of the section. In front of the house is a parking area, and a carport which is almost completely covered by an Albany grapevine. The verandah has roses and wisteria hanging from the eaves, and bog sage, sweet peas and annuals in the beds in front of it.

My letters to you will be about the back garden, a *hortus conclusus* hiding behind a trellis gate that is itself hiding under a rhodo and a fuchsia. When you open the gate, there's a densely cultivated garth of vegetables, fruit trees, roses and flowers. There's also a deck, and a black plastic paddling pool for the exclusive use of the house's large Labrador, Bunsen.

The garden square is 13 metres long and 8 metres wide. Two diagonal concrete paths divide the square into four triangle beds. On the deck are a table and chairs, pot plants, and a pile of bones. To the side of this rectangle, there used to be a small lawn, lovingly laid out by the son of the house. It was to be the deck chair area, a place from which to survey the garden through the gap in the feijoa hedge. As soon as the sprinkler was turned off and the grass established, however, this little lawn was claimed by Bunsen as his en suite.

We are sheltered. The garden is surrounded by corrugated-iron fences, and by the iron roofs of the neighbouring cottages. There are townhouses to the south, a neighbour's tall trees to the north.

Dwarfing all this hangs the long green curtain that is Tinakori Hill to the west. When Parliament is welcoming overseas potentates with blasts on military trumpets, or when Wellington Cathedral's bells peal on Sunday mornings, the sounds reverberate from the hill all around the garden, reminding me of other people's ideas of power and glory. I just go on digging.

Virginia's
Introduction

I feel at a tremendous advantage in this exchange for I have stood in your garden on a balmy summer's morning in February, whereas you have not set foot in mine. Your garden, in my mind, will be forever a summer garden, festooned with rampant growth and vibrating with the chorus of the cicadas. You dared hiss at them to shut up.

There are no cicadas in my garden, a farm garden at Double Tops in the 'hills back of Hawarden' in North Canterbury, elevation 500 metres. The summers are fickle, stalked by rogue frosts and harsh winds. Trees guard the garden from the worst ravages of the prevailing nor'west wind: to the west, old man pine trees and Lombardy poplars; to the east, more poplars; and to the south, tall eucalyptus trees; only the north border is open, to admit the sun. We live inside the barricades in a white weatherboard farm house. The garden is a haphazard mix of shrubs, roses, perennial borders, flaxes, lawns and trees. My favourite, most loved, and most cared-for part of the garden is the vegetable garden where I grow all the vegetables we can eat. To the east of the vegetable garden, a sheltered paddock guards a raspberry frame and a hen house.

Beyond the sheltered paddock and through a little wooden

gate, there is a pond — Kit's pond. The pond is shadowed by flax, cabbage trees, ribbonwoods, lacebarks and kowhais. Mallard ducks and a pair of pukekos loiter at the water's edge. A large rock which we carried in from the hills sits amongst the flax and tussocks. A bronze plaque on the rock faces the sun; it commemorates the life of Kit and the thirteen who died with him at Cave Creek. I can look out my kitchen window, across a tangled bed of shasta daisies, fallen delphiniums and roses, to the rock and the brass plaque. The plaque reflects the light of the sun in the early morning and the pale glow of a full moon at night; I remember Kit as a small boy playing in the duck pond, looking for tadpoles with his dachshund Fritz.

My garden does not stop at the fences and gates that keep the cows and the sheep and the horses from the door; it reaches out to include the whole of Double Tops. I like to think the farm is a large and unruly extension of my garden. The rolling paddocks, the tussock hills and the rocky outcrops, the swampy gullies and the slow-flowing creeks, the remnants of sooty beech forest and the thorny matagouri, I know them and love them as I know and love the managed garden. But, and this is a deep secret, sometimes, when the wind is screaming and trying to suck the hair from my head and I'm spattered with mud, when the cold is freezing my eyeballs and paralysing my hands I wish I lived in the city and drank lattes at brunch.

P.S. We have a house dog as well as our eleven working dogs. His name is Henry, a miniature dachshund. He sends kind regards to Bunsen and has no wish to wallow in the black plastic paddling pool. He has no regard for cats and would kill your cat Tenz if he could.

March

Dear Janice

There was a message on my answer phone at lunch time yesterday. It said, 'I can do tray of twelve, Mrs Pawsey.' It was my friend, Pam. We call each other Mrs Pawsey and Mrs Ewart in March because we are both competing for the 'ribbon'. The ribbon is the championship ribbon in the fruit and vegetable section of the Hawarden A&P show. It is awarded to the most outstanding entry and it is usually bestowed upon the 'collection of not more than twelve vegetables', although one year the ribbon was taken out by a lettuce.

Vegetable growers are phlegmatic people, we move with the rhythm of the seasons, we accept the foibles of nature and of judges. When we take our entries in to the hall supper room we compliment each other on the splendour of our fruit and vegetables and wish each other luck. Vegetable exhibiting is not like the pony ring where tears and tantrums are frequent, and where mothers question the judge's decision. No one in the fruit and vegetables would ever query the judge's decision.

You may not understand this, living in the city where people don't seem to want to know their neighbours, but the A&P show is a big gathering of neighbours where everyone is happy to see each other. Almost everyone at the show is an exhibitor, an official or a stall holder. Harry and I don't exhibit anything apart from my 'tray of twelve' but we are both minor officials. Harry is the gate steward for the Hunter events in the horse and pony rings. I'm the marshal for the terrier race. You would love the terrier race. Mind you, your Bunsen would not be eligible; you do not have to be a terrier to race, but you must be a *small* dog. The race is a mêlée. The terriers line up in the middle of the main show ring with their handlers. A huntsman trots back and forth on a big horse. He tows a dead hare, tantalizing the terriers until they are yelping, salivating and snarling. I signal the huntsman. He gallops away towards the finish line. I lower the start flag and the terriers are off — in all directions. The winners must cross the finish line and be collected by their catchers. Very few terriers cross the line. The race is usually won by Flossie McCubbin-Howell. Flossie belongs to the doctor's family and there is always the suspicion that she is fed steroids from the medicine cabinet, but this has not been proven.

If you want to enter a tray of twelve vegetables you must have at least fourteen varieties of vegetable to choose from. All the usual suspects are there, root vegetables, brassicas, beans, lettuces, plus a few more unusual ones like kohlrabi, Florence fennel, scallopini and tomatoes. Yes, tomatoes.

I will never grow tomatoes as you do. Tomatoes struggle in the hills back of Hawarden. Every year I engage in a battle to pick the first tomato before the arrival of the first frost. This autumn I won, the frost lost the fight: we ate our first tomato last Wednesday, tiny Sungolds — grown from the Kings Seed catalogue. They are like Sweet 100s only apricot orange when ripe — the blackbirds haven't worked out that they are edible yet.

When you live in the country you are always cooking; for visitors, shearers, family, tourists, casual workers. I like to serve fresh vegetables and use what happens to be in season in the garden, so we have runs of vegetables: broccoli, beans, Brussels sprouts, zucchini sixty different ways. Zucchini are like triffids, fruiting relentlessly, growing past eating size within hours. Not everyone likes zucchini and I certainly wouldn't serve them to the shearers day after day.

We used to employ blade shearers who lived in and required huge roasts and puddings, and bacon and eggs for breakfast. We now employ 'electric shearers' who come by the day, so I only make lunch and morning and afternoon tea. Cooking for shearers is one of the great anachronisms of the post-feminist world — many of us still bow to tradition and cook hot savouries, éclairs, sponges, muffins, gems, pizzas and working lunches. I do not begrudge the time spent cooking for the shearers. They work hard, long hours. They are industrial athletes.

The shearers were in for lunch last week. I served my standard shearers' summer lunch, cold corned beef and salad with pickled beetroot, potatoes and peas (Watties frozen) and a choice of basil or sweet Highlander mayonnaise. In the old days the Highlander would have been the dressing of choice, but shearers have, like us all, become more sophisticated in their eating habits. They chose the basil, I was surprised. Here is the recipe.

In the blender put —

1 egg
½ teaspoon of salt
¼ teaspoon of sugar
1 teaspoon of dry mustard
¼ cup of white vinegar
¼ cup of basil leaves

Blend until smooth and creamy then slowly add one cup of canola oil. You can add more basil, but if you add too much the mayonnaise turns a nasty blackish colour, the basil leaves oxidize.

Talking of salads reminds me of the brown whistling frogs. One shearing day I found two frogs sheltering in the outer leaves of the lettuce I'd cut from the garden. They leapt into the sink and began swimming around. Mowing the lawns in spring and autumn I have to watch for little brown frogs. The vibrations of the lawn mower must upset their peace of mind because they leap out of the damp borders into the path of the mower and commit suicide if I don't see them in time. I'm very careful with the little whistling frogs. There are fewer of them than there used to be, I wonder if they have succumbed to the mysterious virus which has led to a world-wide demise of frogs. Once upon a time the night used to pulsate with their singing and now it doesn't.

Dear Virginia

Somehow I don't think office workers' quick lunches are quite the same as shearers' lunches. I have just rushed home this lunch time to do a quick pick-my-own and eat-my-own lunch before rushing back over the motorway bridge to the office.

What shall I graze on? Tomatoes, beans, lettuce, spinach, all the herbs, apples, alpine strawberries, grapes — well no, they aren't there any more. Hmmm. Must choose carefully. There are hazards for the unwary when bushwhacking through the lavender, hydrangeas and those huge nicotianas to find the ripest cherry tomatoes. I might see an oxalis growing where I don't want it and start mad passionate weeding and forget the time. I might see the spinach drooping (it is so hot at midday at present!) and start hosing, and end up with soaked office shoes. No. I'll be focused. My mission is to get lunch. I will do just that. I will not be distracted by the beauty that surrounds me.

A lunch of quickly sautéed, just picked, cherry tomatoes is irresistible after a morning doing monthly project accounts. But do not prick a hot cooked tomato with a fork. If you do, a spurt of scalding tomato lava will spray all over that special white top you chose in the fumbling dawn this morning because today's the important meeting with that difficult client, at 2 p.m.

Later, I change my top, pat Bunsen, and rush back to the great indoors of fluorescent lights and sealed windows, to the formal meeting in the Board Room, with the difficult client. Someone says, during the introductions, 'This is Janice. Er, Janice, is that a cobweb in your hair?'

All the dog owners in my office took their dogs out to the great outdoors, the Pickle Pot sand dune at Paekakariki, for a treat last week. We call it team building. We didn't have bloodied dead hares in our picnic baskets, but we did manage some dog races. Bunsen didn't win. He doesn't understand competition, and the idea of hurrying to get from A to B bewilders him. I mean, his baggy eyebrows say, why would you?

Where did the frogs go??? The only wildlife I've had in my city garden lately has been a bizarre neighbour who has been in the garden gate, while I was away, and shut the cat door from the outside, thus trapping the cat inside. Very strange. Oh, and all the grapes have disappeared. I have consequently wrapped Bunsen's choke chain round the gate post and padlocked the gate shut. I can't imagine you would have these sorts of problems.

Dear Janice

I was terribly sorry to hear of your grape loss. It is the sort of thing intruders do, steal ripe grapes. It must be very hard to protect your crop from human predation in the city. I could send you a .22 rifle and some ammunition but feel our old ferret traps would be a more user-friendly deterrent. The traps come connected to a length of chain. If you suspended the traps by the chain, concealed amongst the leaves, you could catch an intruder by the fingers. It would be a painful but not life-threatening experience for him. My grapes have not attracted any attention yet. They are as green and hard as new peas. The long, hot summer has not come to pass but they may still ripen before the frosts.

The greatest luxury in having a big vegetable garden is to dig new potatoes from Christmas until Easter. I plant them in sequence so there are always tiny new waxy potatoes to eat. I like to boil new potatoes with mint and sea salt, more than we can eat at once, and fry them next day in virgin olive oil until they are brown and crisp. They are to die for — stupid expression, if you die you're not there to eat them.

Green peas are a luxury too. Tiny peas take ages to pod but it's worth the effort, they taste so old-fashioned. I love sweet basil and grow heaps to make pesto and mayonnaise, other favourites are baby beetroot, for shearers' lunches, coriander for Asian cooking and Florence fennel, though I'm not quite sure about Florence fennel. It tastes of aniseed, fragrant in a salad and risotto but the smell of crushed fennel reminds me of derelict houses and despair.

Dear Virginia

Last week, when I took Bunsen to the farm near Paekakariki he stayed on when I went tramping, I stopped at a farm gate and bought four bags of horse manure. You put your $2 for each bag in a jar in the mail box, and it goes to the kids who bag the manure into recycled supermarket bags. I drove home with the bags in the boot, backed the car into the carport, forgot the manure, and went tramping. So there was my hatchback, turning into a compost bin in my sunny carport. Today, my first working day back, I had to visit a recording studio. Dressed in my work clothes I hopped into the car — pooh! It will take more than air freshener to make that car suitable for driving actors and musicians to gigs. I don't imagine you pick up small bags of horse manure at roadside stalls . . .

How did your tray of 12 vegetables go? Did you medal, as they say in the Olympics now?

Dear Janice

Not a medal. In the country it's ribbons. Neither Mrs Ewart nor I won the ribbon. It was awarded to Mrs Bamford's entry in the fruit section, a winning arrangement of apples, pears, berries and grapes, reclining artfully on red grape leaves.

Every time I'm out in the paddocks and I see horse or cow manure I think, two dollars a bag, Janice is paying two dollars a bag! That is expensive. I never use horse manure; it carries nasty weed seeds. Our horses are rather partial to docks. Horse manure is far too much like hard work anyway, as the horses do not deposit it in convenient piles, let alone in carrier bags.

I use sheep manure and you may well comment that sheep do not deposit in convenient piles either, but when they are 'shedded up' in the wool shed overnight awaiting shearing they drop neat little marbles between the gratings. Every few years a contractor arrives with a large vacuum cleaner which sucks out the manure and piles it into a conical sheep poo mountain. In the spring I order a load from the mountain. Harry cranks up the old tip-truck and deposits a ton just outside the garden gate, I barrow it to the vegetable garden. As well as the ton of sheep manure, I order a couple of tons of silage which I use as mulch in the decorative parts of the garden. How far will your horse manure stretch?

P.S. Do you save summer seeds for the next year?

Dear Virginia

Yes. I do collect seeds. A friend gave me the sort of Christmas present that an office worker can create in a few minutes with computer and printer, and a quick raid of the recycling pile at work to find an ideal box, but little did she imagine the amount of work the using of her present would entail. The present was a whole stack of little brown envelopes, top-opening, all filed neatly in a box. On the front of each envelope was a label, to be filled in by me. *Name of seeds*, *colour*, *gathered from*, and *date*. I thought it was a perfect Christmas present, until March rolled round and seed gathering, labelling and filing began to take up more time than I had available in the all-too-short weekends. And it was too much like 9–5 office work. I don't want to bring project management and time allocations back home to the garden.

I like the way Nature packages each variety of seeds differently. Poppies come in round goblet cases with tiny holes round the gathered top so the fine dust-like seed can be shaken out in the wind. Sweet peas come in pods shaped like tiny glasses cases. If you pick them too early the cases are too soft to spring open when pressed. If you pick them too late you find the sun has sprung the pods open, the seeds have gone, and the two sides of the case have twisted into spirals, like DNA filaments. I picked all the sweet pea seed cases, a huge job in itself. Then slowly, whenever there was something interesting on the radio, I pressed open each pod, and shook the seeds into a bowl. It took hours. I ended up with a full bowl. Now I'll have to divide the seed among many of the seed envelopes, fill in the labels, keep some and share some with other people. Going through this exercise made me realize just how labour-saving is a shop-bought packet of seeds.

But nothing beats the return on labour of collecting goblets of poppy seeds from the wild Flanders poppies that sprouted out of the base of an office block on Molesworth Street, sharing them with friends, shaking some into the wind, and waiting and hoping to see Parliament Grounds and the High Court full of poppies next year.

It's never a problem finding people to benefit from the bounty of an over-productive, organic city garden. I live just minutes away from high-rise offices crammed with people to whom a home-grown apple or bunch of grapes is more 'real' than those in the supermarket across the road. When I hand the fruit out, the suited, clean office workers always smell them first.

'Wow!' they say. But they never know the ultimate treat: eating a raw bean from the vine first thing in the morning, in the garden. It is so crisp it snaps like a twig.

I am imagining you coming through the garden gate today. The first thing you see is the narrow path with upright rosemary on one side, and California poppies and wallflowers at its feet. The red rose, Dublin Bay, and Lady Hillingdon, yellow, are on the other side with primulas (not flowering) and bidens, diascia, and lobelia, and chives. The Dublin Bay is always overwhelming, with hundreds of blooms. The narrow path leads through an archway of white stars. It's a perfumed mandevilla which has reached for the plum tree on the other side of the path. The plum has a daphne at its feet.

I'm off to Foxton Beach for a short holiday from work, to do some concentrated writing to meet a deadline. I can never write at home. The garden is too demanding.

Dear Janice

Foxton Beach. How envious I am. Time out at the beach. The thundering surf, sand dunes, a bird sanctuary. In my teens I remember thinking that bird watchers, as described in English country magazines and children's books by Enid Blyton, must be the nerdiest of individuals, and now I enjoy the seasonal comings and goings of the birds in the garden and out on the farm. Labradors love birds too. Killing birds is such fun. Will this be a problem with Bunsen or is he one of those ineffectual bird hunters who never manage to land on the bird when they pounce?

We have lived our lives to the quardle oodle ardle of the magpies. In the autumn they hold a convention in the trees every evening. They give me the creeps, clutching the bare branches and swaying in the wind, quardling as if they know something we don't. People say they chase away native birds, so every now and then I get out the .22 rifle and fire shots into the midst of their conversations and they fly away for a while. Now you can't do that in *your* garden. Imagine the armed offenders unit tramping up to your front door and commanding that you lay down your weapon, only to find themselves confronted by a demented gardener loosing off pot-shots at city pigeons.

The native birds fly down from the bushy hills and gullies in the autumn and forage in the garden. As I write on this first morning of the end of daylight-saving I'm sitting in my 'room of my own' looking out the north-facing windows. The hills are obscured by shrubbery because I do not like to trim the grevillias on account of their being a bellbird treat. I can see three bellbirds loitering amongst the branches of the silver birch tree which they use as a dropping-off station high above the grevillias.

In the autumn I look forward to the arrival of the fantails. They spend their time in the garden pirouetting and diving after flying insects, chatting incessantly, fanning their tails. I have developed a fantail dialect by pursing my lips and sucking through them against my teeth. The fantails flit down and listen, chattering at the same time. They are not programmed to fear us as much as the introduced birds do and they flit dangerously close to people and animals, which is why we do not have a cat. When we were children we believed fantails were the spirits of the dead. Sometimes, when a fantail hovers close, I still like to believe they are.

Dear Virginia

I've just put a pigeon pie in the oven for the dog groomer's lunch. Joke. The only bird excitement here this week was when one neighbour confessed to me that her cat had eaten another neighbour's budgie. We hid by my sunflowers and listened to the bereft neighbour calling for her pet.

Most of the spring and summer colours have gone, as well as the luckless budgie. But of course there are flowers. There are always flowers. Six-feet-tall nicotianas line up along the new back fence. Their Velcro-like leaves aren't very pleasant to walk past. But their perfume is wonderful. And they self-sow. Everything does in this garden, or else it's here for a very short time. If the seedling nicotianas appear in the wrong place, I trowel them out and put them in the row.

I only have time for easy flowers. These include pansies, California poppies, cosmos, lychnis (campion) with white felted leaves and white flowers — I don't like the red campion — shirley poppies, which I keep growing from seed because I love their crinkly delicacy, and tall shasta daisies, and achillea, and roses.

I always have cosmos. I don't control them. They just grow anywhere. At present there's a pink one in the beans, 5 feet tall and in full flower. (Not a very nice colour combination with the red bean flowers.) They take up very little ground space and lots of air space above ground so they are ideal for a small garden in autumn.

As you have lots of space you could let Japanese anemone

and cosmos run wild. They make a lovely match. I did this the first year in this garden. For me, with such a tiny space, it showed no forward-planning at all. Now I am forever pulling out Japanese anemone runners. But they did look lovely that first year, ten years ago, when all I had was a grass and rubble square.

Four white lilies have trumpeted forth, like in Verdi's *Requiem*. I can't remember planting them. They are a little triumph! Only a little triumph because they all face the hill. You open the gate and they stand there, alongside the rosemary walk, with their backs to you. This is not as welcoming as they should be. I think they are regale lilies, Vita's lilies. They might be indicating their dissatisfaction with the very modest garden they find themselves in after pushing upwards through the soil hoping they were blooming in Sissinghurst.

Dear Janice

Over these sultry days of the Indian summer I've worked on the farm in the mornings and gardened in the afternoons accompanied by the chorus of earnest fantail twitter. I cut back some of the perennials, the shasta daisies, catmint, blue scabiosa, garish pink lychnis, sidalceas, they all needed their spent dead-heads removed and their expansion curtailed. Perennials need such discipline, they are not respecters of their less robust neighbours; I am always losing fragile perennials through neglect. You just forget they are there until you find them strangled. I found withered pink cone flowers (*Echinacea purpurea*) beneath the shastas when I cut them back, I was furious with the shastas. It is my responsibility in the garden to be the mediator and I failed.

Dear Virginia

I'm glad you are an angry gardener sometimes too. A huge resentment is growing in me because winter is about to offend me with its short days and cold winds that will rip the tamarillo tree to bits. I get a grip, and go into the garden in a raging 80 k an hour gale and dig over a small perfect bed. I add blood and bone, and compost, and set out seedlings of silverbeet. Then I sprinkle sea mulch around them, which Bunsen and I collected from Petone beach yesterday in perfect sunshine. The sun goes down behind the hill. The wind is rising. I throw myself inside, into a chair and am tempted by garden catalogues advertising bulbs and lilies.

Should I be tempted by those catalogues? Of course. Gardening is all about looking to the future. The minute autumn is on us we are planning for spring. It's about delayed gratification. It's about faith. I get up to iron those shirts for the Monday to Friday business of earning the lily money.

I am not watching my swaying sunflowers. Seven feet tall, and yet to flower, they may not make it through this autumn storm. I don't want to see them fall. They've been great. Their huge heart-shaped leaves have finally blotted out the tall townhouses. I can wander most of the garden in private. And I owe it all to a packet of seeds, and a resulting row of four giant sunflowers. I think next year I'll plant ten of them all along the fence line. Then I can hide behind them and watch for the grape thief.

Dear Janice

I grow my frost-tender plants, zucchini, corn and beans, side by side because if the autumn is malicious and conjures an early frost the plants must be covered with frost cloth. The cucumber, basil and green peppers grow in plastic tunnels. The cucumber plant has grown the length of the tunnel and out underneath the edges and it has produced multitudes of cucumbers, which I have left in the big communal mail box at the end of the road. I hope the neighbours will help themselves.

The scarlet runners have stopped flowering suddenly. A subtle dimming of the sun's intensity must signal the end of the scarlet runner summer. I will let the left-over beans hang out to dry for next year's planting.

It's late, past eleven o'clock, Henry thinks there is a possum in the garden. He's very agitated. There could be a frost, the night is still, the stars are out.

Dear Virginia

At the end of March I like to take a break from the garden, stop being the gardener and become the lady of the manor. I wander the paths. I think each path is about 6 strides long so it isn't arduous. I pick a tomato here, a grape there. An apple (we have a huge number of apples on a very small tree) then a handful of herbs — basil, chives, parsley, thyme. I admire the green tamarillos and feijoas. I wonder when the passionfruit will start passionfruiting. I congratulate the still-blooming Souvenir de la Malmaison, and Dublin Bay. I might or I might not prune the hydrangeas. I gather zucchinis and alpine strawberries. I almost feel I should put the trug over my arm and amble along, filling it. I don't. The trug is on the front verandah, full of last year's acorns. Late summer — Feb/March — to me is time for reaping, not sowing. Sit in the deck chair. Don't stir up the compost. Rest before the major autumn clean-up. I can have these little pauses in a small garden because it's easy to bring control back to the wilderness later.

I have a bucket of tomatoes, and lots of huge dried pods with pink freckled beans in them. I'll make a tomato sauce to store for pastas when I'm in Foxton again next month. And sometime this week I'll have to unburden the little apple tree and make jars of apple sauce. It seems to me that this plot is hugely productive, but it could just be my city person's astonished reaction to what comes out of a fertile piece of ground.

Tell me how my high-country farm is coping with the end of the golden weather.

Hello, Janice

Um, I have to put one thing right, we are hill-country farmers, not high-country farmers. There is a distinction which goes beyond topography. The high-country farmers are legendary characters, wind-blown, hardy. They run fine merinos, they talk about pastoral leases, tenure review and retired mountain tops. They look down upon us farmers of the foothills as mere players in the mustering game. Our musters last hours, theirs last for days. We do belong to the High Country branch of Federated Farmers but we are there to swell the numbers and go to the field days which are held on farms with mythical status like the Molesworth, Rainbow, Mesopotamia. Right, that's straight. I feel less of a fraud.

Dear Virginia

Legendary, wind-blown, hardy, hill-country farmer and grower of amazing cucumbers, feeder of shearers, all done without guidance from Human Resource Managers or staff meetings . . .

At this time of year the profligacy of it all sometimes gets to me. The garden is being invaded, by insects and plants. First there are the tomatoes that have self-seeded right beside the path, and that are all green leaves and few, if any, yellow flowers yet, and the season being so late, what is the point? But I hate to pull things out. I have a huge nicotiana sylvestris, 6 feet high and 4 feet wide, with leaves large enough to make into wrap-around skirts. I love their perfume. I love the fact they are far too big for the garden. I never plant them. I bought one, once, at the Thorndon School fair. I now have enough to give to everyone who goes to the Thorndon fair. Anyway, this one particular nicotiana has placed himself (I feel sure they are hims) right in front of a small, new Graham Thomas, thus blocking all sunlight and sense of the passage of time from the poor rose. But I cannot pull the bully out. It is right in the middle of a pathway made of concrete slabs with gaps between. Usually there are forget-me-nots and heart's ease there but now there is this giant interloper, this nicotiana colonist. I say to myself, he won't last for long. He is flowering. Soon, when the white trumpets and the perfect perfume are gone, I'll pull him out and fight him into the compost bin. But not yet.

This weekend I put the garden to bed — a little earlier than usual this year, and more hurriedly because I was going away on work business. I do manage perfectly well without a tip-truck! I cut down all the beans, prune back all the rampant roses, vines, hydrangeas, ivy (I am constantly invaded by the neighbour's ivy!). I try to control the giant rosemary that seems to think it's a sequoia. OK I know it's a small garden, but huge piles of stuff accumulate. Everything gets piled into the centre of the deck — the compost sorting area. Then, over a period of a week or two, when the stuff is limp and soft, or gone brittle and easy to snap, it gets pushed into the black plastic compost bins. There's one in each corner of the garden, and an extra two round the side of the house. All these are filled. A few days later they are filled again, after the settling-in period. Then a bag of horse manure gets dumped in the top of each bin, with some blood and bone, lime, and two buckets of manure 'tea' which I brew surreptitiously all year. Then the lids go on and that job is over. The deck and paths are swept. Oh I forgot to mention — the old compost (which always reminds me of fruit cake) from the bins has been scattered all over the weeded and emptied soil. The soil and I can relax, eat well, and rest a while.

Nasturtiums have taken over the bed around the tiny lawn. It was meant to be a 'no care' bed with agapanthus (for their perfect blue flowers with that faint stripe of pink in them) in a tangle of nasturtiums. And the straps of the aggies looked so good with the plate-like leaves of the nasturtiums. BUT plants get old and greedy, like humans. The nasturtiums have now reached out nacreous, grasping fingers, right into the lawn. The leaves are speckled and browning: those plates look as though they have last night's stew on them. The plants will have to come out. I manage this act of destruction, and weed underneath them. Below the green dinner plates, convolvulus has been spinning away, under and over the soil. Frustration.

And don't mention borage! Borage is the gardening equivalent of an STD. You are given it by friends. It hides there. You forget you have it. Then suddenly it's spread all over, everywhere.

And it isn't just weeds that are bent on going forth and multiplying. I have so many tomatoes! Buckets of them! I make tomato sauces and soups. The kitchen benches are crowded with onions, beans, parsley, spinach, basil which has gone woody but still has good-smelling leaves, I have to make minestrone, huge pots of it, then decant the soup into jars and store them in the freezer. Will this garden never let me rest!

Black blotches appear on leaves. The leaves turn yellow, then die, then fall off. I know I'm meant to get rid of them. I promise to spray with Bordeaux. But I don't do it. Can't a garden enter autumn gracefully, with resignation? There's powdery mildew on the remaining grapes, and squash. I know that a spray made from baking soda and veg oil (1 tsp of each) and a squirt of soft soap, in a water solution (1 litre) will get rid of this but, hey, it is the season of decay.

And the bugs have arrived. The beans have stopped producing anything edible. Their leaves are a conference venue for green beetles. The catering is of a high standard. On the menu today was bean leaves and tamarillo tree leaves. Someone told me to plant white cosmos near them. The beetles adore white cosmos. But why would I want them on the cosmos? Nah. I leave the minestrone glugging on the stove and rush out to demolish the bugs' convention centre. I pull the bamboo poles out and slide the bean leaves off into a pile. The autumn clean-up has started.

Bunsen decided, yesterday, not to bury the latest bone he's adding to his bone collection. It's on the deck, and has become the lazy, March flies' holiday resort.

The feijoas are ripening and dropping. I want to completely redecorate the tomato areas of the garden. I'm tired of the 'look'. I'm tired of the taste. Roll on, Earth. Let's get to autumn.

April

Dear Janice

April 2nd and it feels like winter, a southerly storm dying reveals the Puketerakis, the mountain range at the end of the road, white with snow. Last night we were sitting ducks for a humdinger frost. At ten o'clock when I ventured out to cover the tomatoes with frost cloth I thought I heard the faint stirring of the pines to the west. But I huffed into the night and my steamy breath rose straight up into the black night air. Straight steam usually means a frost. I covered the whole frost-sensitive vegetable garden with plastic sheeting. The lawn was frozen by midnight but in the morning the wind was up and the garden reprieved.

The roses, into their second or third flowering, are too beautiful to die of frost. I have a New Dawn sprawling over an archway on a garden path. It is usually only able to muster one dawning; this year, due to the summer rain, it is dawning a second time and is covered in pale pink roses. The climber, Bantry Bay, which drapes the swimming pool fence, is a swathe of dark pink. The faithful Dublin Bay climbers are splotched with deep, glorious red roses. They must be the most recurrent flowering climbers ever.

Hardly a week passes at Double Tops without a visit from someone. Nearly all the visitors are men — stock agents, merchandising reps, pig shooters, trappers, farmers and contractors. I hardly ever see another woman. In the old days women used to visit each other to drink cups of tea and eat home-baked biscuits and cake. Today everyone is too busy. So imagine my surprise when Mandy, my very good neighbour and friend, knocked on the back door. She was delivering a new car tyre from John at the garage. I asked her in and we sat and talked, drank coffee and ate chocolate biscuits from a packet. We talked about meeting with city women at city parties, Mandy had just been to a smart city cocktail party. We talked of how, when asked what we do, and we say 'farming', there is a small silence followed by a polite 'Oh.' It is as if you are a person of no consequence, a woman who has never had a career. I said to Mandy, 'Don't worry about it. I have a friend in Wellington who works in a publishing house. She is shut in an office all day labouring under fluorescent lighting, breathing recycled air. Sometimes she writes that she is envious of my work on the farm.' 'But,' asked Mandy, 'has she seen your face?' Mandy has a 'thing' about our faces being savaged by the dry cold wind.

I rushed to the mirror after Mandy had driven down the drive. I looked at my weather-crinkled face and giggled. I didn't really need to look. I have known for years that my skin has never looked like city skin. Men visitors do not create such angst.

Dear Virginia

You can tell your friend Mandy that if I meet someone at a party who says she's a farmer, I'm impressed. Well, actually, I never meet farmers — so separate is the town/country divide. I think of them (you) as free, independent, running a business requiring hard work. Do farmers ever get fired up at goal-setting workshops? Do they bore the shearers with PowerPoint presentations about the farm's mission? Or re-branding meetings? (Our sort of branding is usually a mark on paper, not burnt into skin.) And tell Mandy too that weather-whipped skin is a lot healthier than the pallor of blotchy office skin, which saggily covers a body that is so unfit it depends on osteopaths, chiropractors, physios, masseurs (all on ACC) just to keep it propped up at the desk. All these services are usually before or after lunch, making a nice out-of-office experience for the worker desperate to get up and move away from the fenced-in paddock that is her computer screen.

April is such a different month from March. Suddenly, red grape leaves shingle the garage. The blue colour intensifies in lobelia, pansies, bog sage and sky. Monarch butterflies crowd round the cosmos flowers in the early mornings. The wind arrives. The cosmos, always too tall, blow over. Tinakori Hill becomes a boom-box of roaring sound. It's too dark after work to garden. I farewell the garden on Sunday afternoon and say hello again the following Saturday morning.

After a day in the office in winter the last thing I want to do is garden. I've lost my identity as an outdoor person after eight hours under fluorescent lights. I'd have to change out of uncomfortable office clothes and into a different mindset, before I could plunge into the cold garden. No; that isn't something I can do after a day at the office. After work, the only thing to do with leisure time is to waste it. I curl up with a drink and the mail.

In April weekends I plant poppies, stocks, sweet peas and larkspur; simple flowers that will winter over with no trouble, and colour the garden before anything else can in August and September. There's no need to be complicated, no need to hunt out strange rare species of something.

It's late at night. Must go outside and stamp on a few snails.

Dear Janice

I know it is bizarre, being April, but the tomatoes are in full production, though they did suffer a check with that tinge of frost. We have eaten another meal of green peas and still have open-ground lettuces. The frost blitzed the basil in its tunnel, but didn't harm the coriander. I've not grown coriander in winter and do not know how susceptible to frost it is, but it must have some tolerance because its leaves were frozen stiff and they seem to have thawed unharmed. The tomatoes were only lightly singed under the frost cloth.

Have you ever made harira? It is a very delicious Moroccan lamb soup flavoured with lashings of coriander. I think sheep farmers should all have their own special version of harira, as the Moroccans do. Harira is traditionally eaten during Ramadan, but as we don't have Ramadan I make it as a winter soup. Harira is a good way to use a shoulder of mutton. This is how you make Double Tops Harira.

> Take 300 gms of finely chopped mutton and
> brown it in a pan, remove, then fry two chopped
> onions along with five cloves of garlic. Cook until
> the onion is transparent then add 1 tsp cinnamon,
> ½ tsp of ginger, ½ tsp cumin. Fry a little bit more,
> then add one large, finely chopped carrot, black
> pepper and some saffron if you are extravagant.
> I add fresh roasted and crushed coriander seeds
> from the garden instead of the saffron.
>
> Next, put the mutton and the onion mixture into a
> pot and add 3 litres of stock (chicken or mutton)
> and two 440 gm tins of tomatoes, crushed. Of

course if you have your own tomatoes, fresh are better. Boil for about 2 hours.

When the mutton is tender, add a can of chick peas — drained — and 150 gms of lentils. Cook a further ½ hour or until the lentils are mushy. I like to leave the harira overnight at this stage to let the flavours blend. Before serving, reheat and add about 3 tbs fresh coriander and 2 tbs of parsley, Italian is best but the crinkly kind is OK too. Before serving, add the juice of a lemon, and salt to taste. You can also add more cumin if you want. I serve the harira with warm flat bread. Moroccans eat it with figs, dates, nuts and other delicacies.

We have an army of pest exterminators patrolling the farm this month. Target Pest are cyaniding possums. This did not deter two possums from attempting to forage in the garden last week. Henry knows instantly a possum enters the garden. He rushes outside, runs the possum up a tree then stands under the tree barking his head off. Very annoyingly, the minute he hears anyone coming he stops barking. You have to flounder around with a torch trying to locate him, then you have to locate the possum amongst the branches. It's much easier now that the trees are losing their leaves. For years I made Harry go out into the night to shoot the possum, but recently I decided that was pathetic, especially when taunted with 'Girls can do anything, can't they? You go and shoot the bloody thing.' It's a bit of an act lining up the possum in the sights and trying to hold the torch beam in line with everything at the same time. My first attempts used an enormous amount of ammunition and shredded lots of leaves and sky, but the most recent possum dropped straight from the tree after only three shots.

Did you know that it is a common sight, during warm summer nights, to find naked farmers shooting possums off house roofs and trees? Poor mad possums; they are such cute little creatures. You have to harden your heart; their eyes are so big and round and pleading. But they carry TB and eat birds.

Dear Virginia

Hmmm. Small furry animals. I like them. You probably should know that I was very distressed today to find that I'd brushed a praying mantis off my skirt and broken one of its legs. I thought it was a pruned rose cane clinging there. I don't think I'm ready for possum-shooting stories. You should also know that my cat has finally understood that I don't want him to kill birds or even mice. I gave him a toy mouse to play with. He bites at it while his back legs rake back and forth. Horrible. The pet mouse is made of sheep skin.

Dear Ms Marriott

We regret to inform you that your recent request (and utmost desire) to become a farmer in some future incarnation has been declined. We have examined your performance in your present life and have found nothing to indicate that you would be in the least suited to the rigours of killing things. Indeed, killing things is of the essence in a farming career. Farmers must be familiar with, and able to kill, insects, parasites, worms, fungi, weeds, trees, rabbits, ferrets, magpies, geese, sheep, cows, lambs, calves, pigs, deer, swamps and members of the Labour Party.

Yours ever so regretfully . . .

Dear Janice

I was driving home in the dark last week when two cavorting rabbits were lit by the beams from my headlights. They looked so sweet. I drove on swerving neither right nor left; I felt two small muffled thuds. I felt no regret, only satisfaction that the two sweet rabbits were no longer alive to breed another day. You would have swerved to avoid hitting first one, then the other, rabbit. You may well have lost control of the car in the shingle on the side of the road and slid or rolled horribly, over the fence and into Barry O'Carroll's paddock. You wouldn't have been the first person to have rolled into Barry's paddock, but you would have been the first to do so whilst avoiding a rabbit. All the others have been drunks.

No, you would not make a farmer, but, on the other hand, things change when your food supply or your livelihood is threatened. I mean look at you stamping on snails; it's just bloody genocide. It takes great strength of character to sit and watch sweet baby rabbits eating all your newly planted lettuces and corn.

The lawn is dented and damaged with hoof prints. My horse and Fleur's pony came visiting during the night, in through the back gate to graze the lawn. Horses enjoy eating lawns. Harry and I are arguing as to who left the gate open.

Dear Virginia

I have been mustering and feeding out my front-step plants. FSPs have to look good, and flower and flower. I have hostas there in the summer and polyanthus in winter because I love the way their leaves fill the pot and hang over the edge, hiding it completely. Then, from this bed of thick, sleek foliage (if the snails haven't discovered it) rise long stems with mauve, fragrant flowers. This continual meeting and greeting of visitors is exhausting work for FSPs. I wouldn't expect them to be on duty all year round. Like receptionists, they need holidays to sleep in. By April the hostas are looking spent, so today I removed the plants from the pots.

All gardens, no matter how small, need a nursery bed, and a bed for sleeping over. Mine is along a boundary fence at the side of the house. The bed is narrow; it borders an area where cars park. It is frost-free, undisturbed, and covered with mulch from the leaves of the tall silver birches that shade and shelter it. This is where the hostas go for rest and recreation over the winter. This is my big plant muster. They snuggle into their hide-and-sleep bed, as oblivious to winter as a bear in a cave.

Out of this soft, dry, humus-rich bed I take the primulas, polyanthus and cyclamens which have been dry-shading all summer. I plant some along the borders which are now bare, waiting for bulbs to come up. And some I pot up for the front steps. New soil, blood and bone, a good watering, and in a few weeks these rather raggedy leaves will grow into a strong, wrinkled lime green rosette and yellow flowers will appear.

Dear Janice

My garden is awash with mellow yellow and orange as autumn dies. The roses flower with an intensity you don't see in the spring or summer. The blooms are luxuriant, the pink and the orange roses almost luminous. Bantry Bay's summer blooms are now pale orange hips which look vaguely wrong amidst the deep pink autumn flowering. The vegetable garden, which has suffered a few frost scares, is bountiful. April has been balmy, sunny, euphoric. The tomatoes are still ripening and we are still eating green beans which survived the frost burn. The beans all look like piglet tails. Beans and cucumbers do not grow straight in cold weather. They curl up, just like people do when it is cold. The strawberries are ripening; autumn strawberries taste more 'strawberryish' than spring strawberries. It's been a strange old season.

Last week two small rabbits took up residence in the garden and Henry spent his days in a delirium of rabbit hunting. The rabbits did not take Henry seriously, much to their cost. He eventually ran them both to ground and ate them up. More possums have been visiting at night to eat the crab apples in the front paddock; I send Henry and Harry out to deal with them. When Harry shoots the possum it falls out of the tree dead as a doornail whereupon Henry bravely pounces and ferociously 'kills' it all over again, by the tail. Possums are not safe to tackle head on even when they're dead! Last week a wild pig passed briefly through the garden, ate the winter silverbeet and pulled a few leeks.

Dear Virginia

No possums, no rabbits, no horses and no pig. Just a cat and a dog, and wild unwanted people treading where they shouldn't in the garden beds, hunting for basil, thyme, coriander under the invading borage, then scurrying back to their cottages.

I cut back perennials, like lavender, bergamot and catmint, divide campanulas, and end up with hundreds of small plants to give away. Primulas, polyanthus, felicia, penstemons — all get a number 2 haircut. Some get dug up, torn into small plants, and given away, along with plants of self-seeded campion (which is everywhere) and borage (which is everywhere else).

The thyme has crept and colonized all summer and I dig it out, select just one small piece for potting up for the winter, and leave the rest, a huge mound, on the garden bench for people to help themselves to. Gardeners have to give away many plants in autumn or compost them. You don't have to buy plants; just swap them with other gardeners, or turn non-gardening friends onto gardening with a pot of pansies, lobelia, and a scented geranium cutting.

There's always lots of heart's ease in the garden, between the cracks in the pathways, around the trunks of trees, and hidden by the California poppies. Parsley is seeding everywhere. Where the old sage died, hundreds of tiny sage seedlings have sprung up. What will I do with all these potential plants? I don't know. But nature is prolific. Plants are there for the giving and taking. Give and take them. It's a necessary part of the gardening cycle.

In spring I grew seeds of chilli peppers (Hearts variety) to give away as Christmas presents. Now, everywhere I go, my friends have their chilli Hearts plants, on window sills, beside sinks, even in bathrooms. What we are all going to do with so many chillis, I don't know! And all those new seeds!

I must admit, though, that I do often want a little something else. At the moment it is the blue-leafed hosta. My hostas have ordinary green leaves. I want a blue one because it would match the colour of my house. Gardeners can be like this.

I only plant food I like to eat, and that bugs don't like to eat. So in April I have three small patches of silverbeet, one patch a few weeks older than the next, planted in squares. Some are red stemmed and some white. It isn't precision planting like Rosemary Verey's fantasy potager in England. The pattern is more hit and miss than that. Little tatsois are growing in the shade under the late tomato bushes, which are still flowering. Spinach grows proudly in a row, lush and bright green. Rocket grows anywhere. Rocket is a very easy, no-fail, cold-season crop. Winter lettuce lines up in front of the spinach. And if I have time I will plant a row of peas.

Dear Janice

When we first moved to the Virginia road my new neighbour, Adrienne Rutherford, invited me to ladies' tennis. I stayed afterwards for a cup of tea. She had two pieces of advice for me. The first was to always plant my broad beans on Anzac Day, and the second to drive on the road as if there were always a huge sheep truck round every corner. They were valuable pieces of advice. I have always tried to adhere to the second but seldom honoured the first. It is not often you get a second chance if you smack into a sheep truck round a blind corner, but there is a degree of latitude in the time for broad bean planting. I still intend to plant the broad beans before the winter. The seed is in the pantry and the autumn is warm. The other wintering-over vegetable I plant for spring harvesting is broccoli. All other vegetables must be well established by the beginning of winter because there is very little growth. Sometimes the carrots and parsnips must be chipped from the frozen ground and if you don't pick your silverbeet before dusk it will be frozen hard.

Dear Virginia

I will plant broad beans this year, and I will look out for sheep trucks on my drive. We are still picking tomatoes and more and more tomatoes. Some become soup. Lots become dinners. Lots are eaten fresh and new, smelling warm and sunny in sandwiches and salads. They are easy to pick. There's the flare of crimson, as noticeable as a redcoat at the Charge

of the Light Brigade. And when you can't see them because they are deep inside the bush and you are feeling around under the leaves, you can feel the ripe ones from the unripe. The ripe ones are warm.

Peas and beans are always hard to see, because they are green, so I pick them by feel, by the weight in the pods. Every time I've picked the beans, I could return to the garden and pick another bag of ones I've missed the first time. When I cut the beans down I find, hiding behind leaves, huge dry pods I missed long ago. Those old pods aren't wasted. The big, speckled purple bean seeds inside are delicious in soups.

We don't pick feijoas from the trees. (There are four trees.) We pick them up from the ground. That way we know they will ripen, in a bowl. After just a few days they are ready to eat. Their fragrance is intense, and scents the whole cottage.

I picked the last red apple, huge as a cat's head. We are looking forward to one of the best autumn treats: a fresh, home-grown apple. I cut it and slice it thinly. Such white flesh. We eat it with cheese.

'An apple without cheese is like a kiss without a squeeze.' Someone in the family used to say that when I was a child.

I thought it was a good idea to make bean frames from thin branches I cut from trees last autumn. And they did look nicer, more rustic, than the bamboo that you buy at garden centres for a few cents each. But how hard it is to remove the spent bean haulms from those rustic branches! With bamboo you just yank it out of the ground and then slide all the bean plant, leaves, twining stems, the lot, along the bamboo and off — like casting off in knitting. But with those rustic branches, with all their little bumps where the side twigs started from, there's no smooth sliding of any beans to be cast off onto the bean pile. No. It is an unpicking job, long, and tedious, while a chill wind whips round you. I won't be going for the rustic bean frame look next year.

Dear Janice

Last week was pure autumn, crisp blue skies, the smell of sooty mould on the beech trees and the manuka scenting the still air out in the back hills. There is no smell quite like it; mouldering grapes and dark honey come close. There are clouds of wasps and bevies of bellbirds harvesting the nectar.

The sunlight from the more northerly sun makes the sheep glow creamy pearl as they string away through the tussock. The cabbage tree leaves on the bush edge glisten and the hill grasses are dull gold. I was driving down the Double Tops track yesterday and scanning the south Mjølfjel face for stragglers. I spotted a sheep, a large sheep, too large, so I stopped and put the binoculars on it. The 'sheep' was the top tufts of a cabbage tree catching a shaft of sunlight. As the rays slanted over the ridge, the cabbage tree was transformed into a ball of light, a sheep to the naked eye, and then it was gone as the sun travelled on.

Further on down the track, a falcon landed on a post. I stopped and got out of the Toyota, crept close and peered at it. She was an aristocrat, she stood on the post with her brown wings folded, she stared at me with an unblinking brown eye. I stared back. I almost gave up breathing. I crept closer. She spread her wings and glided to the next post, showing wing undersides speckled cream and brown. I crept towards the next post. She spread her wings again and shot into the sky like a rocket then floated away on the wind. I would love to be a falcon.

Must go and cook tea. The desk thermometer says it is one degree outside. There has been a light fall of snow and the lawn is white in the window light. It'll be a cold night.

Dear Virginia

In autumn my hunter-gatherer gene is activated. I forage far and wide. I beg the hairdresser for a bag of hair. The beach is pillaged for kelp, sea lettuce, sea mulch. We gather pine needles before the rains come and make them wet and hence too heavy for the plastic bags. Leaves under a friend's deciduous tree are fair game. I pester friends who turned their backs on inner-city lattes and went to a lifestyle block. 'Could I gather some horse manure from your front paddock?' The boot of the car becomes soggy and smelly. Lime is bought. Blood and bone is stored on the front verandah, out of the way of dogs. Bunsen can smell blood and bone six inches down, so there's no point digging it into the garden unless I want the section rotary hoed by Bunsen's paws. I confine it to the compost bins.

Four of the six bins sit in each of the four corners of the garden, tucked behind grateful trees. They are black plastic, matching Bunsen's paddling pool. How's that for garden design? They have to have lids so Tenz, the cat, can sit on them.

When the main autumn clean-up is done and the lids are shut, one quarter of the garden is left fallow for the winter, and any kitchen scraps and winter green material is dug directly into this bed. In the spring the sweet, crumbly, wormy composts will be ready.

Mulching moments. We are walking the dogs on the beach, with friends. We're having serious conversations about the way the world is going. Suddenly all this stops because I have to fossick through parka pockets for a supermarket plastic bag or two (or three or four, if I can persuade friends to carry them). Why? Because I can't resist a patch of slimy yellow seaweed. It has to be gathered. It can't go to waste. I am doomed to spend the rest of the dog walk striding along swinging bulging supermarket bags of seaweed. This is a mulching moment.

After the walk, it's time to go inside and eat.

Pasta with Sage Sauce

Sauté 4 cloves of sliced garlic in oil.
  Do not overcook.
Add 2 tbspn butter and half a cup of
  small fresh sage leaves.
Cook till they crisp up. Pour over a
  pound of thin, cooked, pasta.
Add black pepper, salt, parmesan.
  Toss.

Nearly Anzac Day. All the recently dug-over beds (which had tomatoes, silverbeet or pumpkins in them) are covered with precise little cosmos seedlings, about 2 inches high, orderly, spaced like war graves. Lilies and irises are torpedoing through the soil, their cones now above the ground, like little rockets waiting to be launched. They look tough and invincible, compared with the delicate California poppies and lobelia around them.

Hello, Janice

Yesterday we were driving down the lane towards home when I spotted Doris. Remember Doris, the aggressive Charolais pet calf? Doris had a friend grazing alongside her rear hooves — I watched, and the bird and she definitely had a relationship. The bird was pure white with a yellow beak, a heron. I knew it couldn't be an Okarito white heron lost on the wrong side of the hill, so I rang Dugald next door. He said it would be a cattle egret. They're Australian visitors and like grazing with cows. I regret the egret has not been back. Maybe Doris was unfriendly. She is not a tolerant cow.

Your calf, your namesake Janice, has grown her winter coat already and looks like a strawberry-blonde yak without horns. I am such a sucker, I keep buying calf pellets for her at twenty-five dollars a bag, I love hearing her mooooooooo every night when I feed the dogs. She and her pal Wallace, the sheep, eat a bowlful of pellets most nights.

I have to go and mow the croquet lawn. Doesn't that sound grand? We have a croquet lawn out at Tommy's Cabin. Tommy's Cabin is the emotional heart of the farm. It has played a big part in our life at Double Tops. Someone said it was built about 1870 as a boundary rider's hut or an outback shepherd's hut. There have always been rumours of a murder at the cabin. Kit and Fleur loved frightening visiting children with tales of a gruesome murder and the ghost.

We used to picnic at Tommy's Cabin when the children were small. There are two small streams that meet at the cabin; gravel streams with eels and bullies, in summer green-leaved willow branches shade the sluggish water. The cabin has two rooms, one has a big open sod fireplace with a chain and a hook to hang a billy; the rimu plank walls are dark with smoke. There is only one tiny window making it difficult to read the newspaper-lined ceiling; the paper is stained and peeling. The old papers advertise strange medicinal remedies like chlorodyne and De Witt's cure for sciatica, 1925-vintage box-shaped Studebaker cars, Remington repeater rifles, Teofani cigarettes, 'useful aprons' and 'simple frocks'. The walls are scratched with the names and the legends of hunters; 'three hares, one pig, two dozen blowflies', or 'one sore foot, two ducks, one hare, three mushrooms'. There are the scribbles of Fleur and her Pony Club friends in 1989. Harry and his brothers and I signed the wall in 1978, the year we bought Tommy's Cabin and the Mount Lance block back from the Lawrence family. Kit was a little baby. I suppose we thought, back then, that he might one day farm Double Tops and bring his own children to picnics at the cabin.

Tommy's Cabin is the home of the Tommy's Cabin Croquet Club, hence the croquet lawn. We play on what we believe are the only tussock croquet lawns in the world. The number one lawn is becoming a little too manicured and we are considering replanting the tussocks, but the number two lawn is very wild. The club meets about four times a year. Every summer we hold a mock annual general meeting to re-elect the office bearers and to set the club playing rules. The rules are fiercely debated, particularly foot on or foot off the ball in the roquet.

The Tommy's Cabin Croquet Cub is to meet on Sunday at Tommy's Cabin for the last match of the season. Tomorrow I'll take the lawn mower out to the cabin and mow between the tussocks. We always have a dress code for our matches. On Sunday it's Russian, pre-revolution; everyone has been asked to bring caviar and black bread, pashka, blinnis; I'm making a big cauldron of borsch. We shall take vodka too, drink shots and smash the plastic glasses over our shoulders into the fireplace shouting 'yavo'. (We will recycle the plastic afterwards.)

One summer we hosted a wedding party at Tommy's Cabin. We decked out the bedroom as the bridal suite; we pushed the two wire beds together to make a double bed with white sheets and a floral duvet. We arranged flowers, candles, chocolates and champagne. Where there are weddings there are funerals; we've held a funeral at Tommy's Cabin too. Kit's funeral.

There was never a question about the funeral venue. Tommy's Cabin was Kit's favourite place when he was growing up. We never considered that it might rain. It didn't. The funeral day was a windless, golden autumn day. During the service the willow trees dropped wizened orange and yellow leaves into the stream. They made no sound. The sky was bright blue. There is a green clearing at the front door of the cabin and everybody stood in a big circle on the grass. The clearing was full of more people than have ever stood there before. At the end of the farewell, Kit's friends carried him away over the Cabin Stream and up the hill as Ariana Tikao sang a waiata. Her voice floated through the willows behind us, haunting and beautiful. It is a moment in time that remains forever. Kit's last leaving of Tommy's Cabin. We never imagined the end of his childhood would be so absolute.

May

Good evening, Janice

Today Harry let Henry out of the Toyota. We were mustering cows and calves in the furthermost corner of the farm. Henry always comes along for the ride when we are mustering. He sits on my knee with his head out the window and snaps at matagouri branches as we drive by. Sometimes he catches a branch, which must hurt him because the prickles draw blood on the inside of his mouth. He is an idiot. This does not endear him to Harry. Anyway, today I was assigned the bottom beat which, as we were driving on the high track, involved a very long, steep walk to the bottom. I left Henry in Harry's tender, responsible care and Harry let him out on the top of a one-thousand-metre hill, twelve kilometres from home, a long way for a miniature dachshund to walk home. After Harry let Henry go, Henry went hunting. I heard his 'pursuit bark' away above me in the bush, the frantic squeaky yapping that alerts the prey he is on the case, which of course is why he never catches anything. When we had finished mustering the block and pushed the cows through the gate, I called Henry. He did not come. We drove home.

It is midnight now. I have twice driven out in the dark, along the track to the Milo gate and then along the Virginia road in case he runs home the way we went out. No Henry. Already the night is frozen, the moon is full, and frost glitters on the grass. It is very spooky alone in the night with the moon casting long, dark shadows in the valleys and lighting up the cabbage tree fronds like clusters of steel swords. Logic tells you that you are alone. Imagination conjures invisible companions stalking the night. At home Harry is fast asleep. He won't care if the 'little bastard' never comes back. I will not forgive him if my little dog doesn't return.

Dear Virginia

I hope Henry came home.

Duck shooting has begun. This doesn't affect me in the office, or the garden, but it did lead to confusion about Bunsen's role when we were in Taumarunui on Saturday, having a coffee at Rivers Two. Guys were walking up the main street in waders. On the back of a parked flat-bed truck, three Labradors: one golden, one brown and one black. A guy in a Swanndri tells me he's sure Bunsen's looking keen. I don't tell him Bunsen is only keen on the lattes and cake on our café table.

On the drive home, poplars were orange or yellow walls of dancing colour. I felt elated by the leaves whirlpooling, spiralling on the roads. I stopped at Pukehou, north of Waikanae, and bought climbers, and a *Viburnum burkwoodii* because I like the red autumn leaves and look forward to the scent of the white snowballs in spring. When you open the garden gate it will be one of the first things you see and smell. I arrived home in the dark. Tomorrow after work, in the dusk, I will garden!

Dear Janice

I don't know how to tell you this and I hope it does not come as a great shock to you and Bunsen, but Bunsen is not a real Labrador. We have a real Labrador living next door. His name is Buzz. Real Labradors go duck shooting and all that sort of stuff. But do tell Bunsen that I have always had a preference for pretend Labradors, who hunt under café tables.

Apropos of Henry, we returned to the scene of Harry's neglect before the sun had melted the frost the next morning. Henry was crouched, silent, amidst the frozen tussocks. He was not surprised to see us, only rather puzzled we had taken so long to return. He assumed his position on the front seat of the Toyota and spent the morning snapping at matagouri bushes whilst we drove a small herd of cows all the way back to the homestead paddocks.

The first weeks of May at Double Tops have been unseasonably warm and bountiful. May is the principal mating month for sheep. The rams indulge in speedy dispassionate sex with 100 ewes apiece. The Corriedale rams were set loose amongst the hill sheep on Anzac Day. The shearers say that hill-country farmers wouldn't know when to put the rams out if it wasn't for Anzac Day. The Oxford and Dorset rams have been 'at it' for a while now. They began their assignment with the paddock ewes on April 9th, Harry's birthday, another useful milestone in the farming calendar. And, the differentiation: hill sheep are young; paddock sheep are old.

Regards to Bunsen.

Dear Virginia

A work-mate's wife died today, leaving a 3-year-old son. In the garden was one perfect camellia. It was creamy pink, with open petals and with a coil of unfurled petals jutting out from the centre. You could see only pink. The yellow stamens were hidden. It was a beautiful thing to stare at for a long time. It was all about swirl, and drapery, and yet it was completely still. It could have been carved out of butter. The next day, when I went to pick the camellia for him, I noticed two petals had brown edges. It was imperfect, and hence wouldn't be the symbol I had wanted for him. Nature is always moving on. Perfection lasts a very short while in the garden, as in life.

Dear Janice

Yes, perfection is transitory. Robert Browning said, 'What's come to perfection perishes.' In the garden you have to enjoy the budding of a flower and the slow opening, for once it is fully bloomed it will begin to brown and die. I'm sorry about your friend's wife. People who die young are like flowers picked too soon from the garden. I don't much enjoy picking flowers.

In late autumn the afternoon sun turns the hills deep gold; against the flat blue sky they are Graham Sydney hills, aloof and still and very beautiful. On Thursday afternoon my dogs and I had to negotiate our way down a steep rock-strewn ridge to the valley floor, sweeping up any cows we found along the way. We discovered four black cows and their calves halfway down. They had been chased from the top bush by Harry's dog, Sydney, and were harassed and irritable. I stood on a rocky knob and sent Toby and Tan down to move them on. Sydney heard the barking and rushed back to assist, I yelled at him to 'piss off'.

The cows decided to make a stand. A cow with a calf is

a cantankerous beast. You have to employ psychology or use brute force to get cows to move if they decide they are not going to be moved. Brute force is a macho man's game needing a team of big, noisy huntaways to pulverize the cows into submission. I have one timid huntaway, Tan, one handy dog, Toby, and two heading dogs, Muffin and Pixie. The psychological option is usually my only option. This involves tactical manoeuvering. I send the dogs down to chase the cows. The cows stand their ground. The dogs dive, bark, and snap, the cows charge, snort and bellow, and concede not one inch of ground. After a suitable time has elapsed, I call the dogs off. The cows think they have won the battle. They decide to move of their own accord. They think they are getting away. They begin to trot down the hill. Sometimes they break into a full plunging joyful gallop, tails stuck in the air.

This tactic didn't work on Thursday. I had to climb down to the battlefield and talk severely to the cows. The stroppy old tarts stood looking at us and swishing their tails. I told the dogs to sit well out of the way. Dogs make cows very peevish. I waved the mustering stick at the cows and I growled and charged at them. The cows grudgingly waddled away round the side of the hill looking very disgruntled. There is no animal can look more petulant and put-upon than a black Aberdeen Angus cow who does not want to leave her territory.

My dogs and I reached the valley floor via a stand of beech, following a stock trail through the trees — black beech and honeydew territory. The trees smelt sour and sweet in the same breath, like fermenting grapes in an over-ripe vineyard. The soot-encrusted trunks and branches of the trees were crawling with bees and wasps harvesting tiny honeydew balls.

Beneath the bush, encamped around a stream's swampy delta, the mobbed cows and calves watched our approach; the aggressive mothers patrolled the outer defensive circle. My dogs and I launched a concerted push on the rear of the mob and we told them sternly it was time for moving out. Reluctantly, herding the calves and muttering to themselves, the cows plodded off up the track. We plodded along behind, the dogs mincing around on tiptoes waiting for the word to hasten the ascent.

Dear Virginia

My stock trail on a cold May day takes me from the fridge to the couch. I read your letter about you mustering rugged hill blocks while I was snuggled into the couch cushions. I'm reading a lot of English gardeners at the moment. I read of them setting off into their gardens, as encumbered with life support accessories as the average commuter. Christopher Lloyd goes into his garden with his tools, in a trug, in one hand and a small iron-framed bed, complete with two blankets, in the other. This bed is for his Tulipa, his dachshund. When the dog's tired of smelling around, she curls up on the bed, under the blankets, hidden from prying visitors. Have you thought of taking beds for the sheepdogs on your muster? I also think of people at work preparing to go into a long meeting: taking their drink bottle, their high-energy snacks, and still waiting anxiously for the catered coffee and chocolate fudge squares at morning tea.

In my small, square town plot, bordered by rusting iron fences, overlooked by stucco townhouses, I have no need for working dogs. Bunsen is part of the perennially unemployed. Nor am I strong enough to carry Bunsen's carved oak double bed outside for him. I can't wander along paths into new spaces, a 'succession of privacies' as they call it at Sissinghurst. I simply come through the garden gate, stand on the practical deck, and there it is, all of it, in front of me. (Well, except for the little lawn/en suite round the corner, but that is hardly worth oiling up the wheelbarrow for, or revving up the Toyota.)

Instead of describing a muster, I thought I'd tell you about paths. I know a path takes you from one place to another, but in gardens the journey is more important than the destination, so paths are different from pavement and roads. They don't have to go directly to the compost, the washing line, whatever. They can wander. They need to be treasures in themselves.

When I moved here there was a square of grass, with one ancient plum in one corner and one apple in the other. The apple was waist-high and leaning like the more famous tower. My priority was to dig up all the grass and make paths that would give access to all parts of the garden. In a small, highly productive garden, you don't want to be trampling on the soil. I decided on a St Andrew's flag pattern. All paths would meet in the middle. There would be four beds, each triangular in shape. Small brick paths would cross the wider parts of the triangles, just one or two bricks wide, just to give access to the plants, for weeding, picking, &c.

So I got the paths laid; that is, I hired someone to do it and I lolled on the couch and read about paths. I read that the English gardener Margery Fish, after her husband had laid a beautiful courtyard of paving slabs, attacked it with a crowbar, cracking the stone so plants would grow between, beside, and within the stones. My paths are concrete. They are uninspired. They are the result of needing to start making a garden and going about it too quickly. I don't wholly dislike my paths. They are practical. I can walk barefoot on them first thing in the morning in summer. They are hardly noticed now that plants grow over them, often meeting in the middle and forming a barrier. But I think I should re-lay the paths in a different pattern and have a rectangular vegie garden in the middle.

Dear Janice

The last big job in May is the mustering down of the hill ewes for the ram change-over. All month the ewes have been slowly moving towards the front blocks. We muster the furthermost blocks by vehicle and foot and the front blocks by horse. It is as quick to muster by horse if you like horses. We like horses. We don't like motorbikes.

Harry came in after feeding out and asked, 'Do you want to take old Tonto out for a ride today? We'll straggle South Phipps and Top Block.' (My horse is named Lady but Harry likes to call her 'Tonto' in a derogatory kind of way.) The wind was shrieking a bit but I nodded. 'Could be worse tomorrow,' I said. We saddled up. Harry saddled Bruno, who was once named Bruiser. All Harry's horses are big and high-spirited. We let the dogs go and rode out into the wind. Up the road the gusts blew little willy willies in the shingle. I pulled my hat down hard on my head but still felt the brim flapping and the brim rim tugging my ears. Lady skittered about with the wind up her tail. She likes to be in front so we cantered off and left Harry exerting grim control over Bruno who thought he should be in the lead.

The wind let us alone in the valleys. We trotted along looking for sheep. Straggling a block involves gathering stray sheep left behind in previous musters or catching up with sheep who have crawled through a hole in a floodgate in the dry months. We had a small mob gathered when we parted company. Harry rode south. I rode west to open the West Phipps gate in the saddle. The wind over the saddle bit through my jacket, vest, jersey, shirt and singlet, froze my fingers, sucked the words from my mouth, blew them away in the wrong direction. We waited for the sheep to run through the open gate, with Harry's Rock in hot pursuit. The sheep decided to crash through the fence halfway down. We shut the redundant gate behind us. I ran Tan up the fence line. Huntaways bark as they run so the sheep soon strung out, noses to the wind, down a sheep track to the valley floor.

We rode on along the top negotiating matagouri thickets, rock rubble and the wind. I had to dig my heels hard into Lady's flanks to force her to climb ridges she didn't want to climb. Horses don't like cold, roaring winds either. My lips lost sensation in the cold and wouldn't hold the dog whistle tight. I couldn't force a whistle out of it and had to use one hand to reinforce the blowing tension and the other to keep Lady headed in the right direction as well as holding my hat on. On blustery days you must use your legs to stay tight in the saddle else you might be sucked off and blown away over the hills and out to sea.

Harry has a legendary optimism in relation to the amount of time required to muster the hill blocks. 'We won't be needing a lunch,' he said, so I didn't make a lunch. By four o'clock I wished I had. A cup of tea and a biscuit would have been nice. A cold half an hour later we left the sheep to overnight in a twelve-acre holding paddock and rode home with the wind at our backs. A wind in the back is warmer than a wind in the face.

Dear Virginia

No lunch while working! That's a Health and Safety issue! I can see the Allstaff email from Human Resources in our company right now:

> We draw all our employees' attention to the Policy document — Lunch — in the Policies folder, where it states that no employee shall work an extended period without a break.

Back in Wellington after another weekend away. Bunsen and I collected 'sea mulch' from Petone Beach on the way back home — two supermarket bags full, which I scattered on the mail-shed bed. I have a newly painted mail shed at the bottom of my drive, but I miss the jasmine that the painters trampled to death in the process. How could you not see a jasmine? Especially as it was about to flower?

The weekend gardening hasn't been done! It's late Sunday afternoon and this is all the time I have for gardening. I rush into it, overwhelmed by the feeling there is too much to do. I will never be on top of this garden. I rip out chickweed. It is everywhere. How do you let sweet peas self-seed (as mine all have) if they are inextricably entangled with that chickweed? Half the sweet peas came out while I attempted to remove the weed. I raged against the dying of the light. I worked too fast, too furiously. It never pays to do this in a garden.

And finally, with regret, I pulled the last tomato plant out of the ground. I took all the unripe tomatoes inside. They will ripen quickly. After I started with that tomato, in the dusk, I couldn't stop. Not exactly a scorched earth policy operating here, but definitely a defoliant approach. With my bare hands, I grasped the last twiggy cosmos tree and heaved it onto the pile. I'm always amazed by the tiny root ball on a cosmos. Where does all that energy come from to make a 5' high cosmos tree? A twiggy daisy bush followed. I broke off a branch for taking hardwood cuttings, for next year. And then it was the turn of the nicotianas, armfuls of struggling nasturtiums, hydrangea heads, dill, clumps of old shasta daisies. The pile grew. I dug a moat round the pile and shovelled soil from the moat onto the top of the pile. Every day for the next month I'll add kitchen scraps to the moat and cover them with soil. The soil on the top of the pile will help it rot down. When it's much smaller I'll dig it all in.

In the dark I planted the viburnum I bought last week, and poppies and salvia. And it was a lot more fun than unpacking the groceries.

Gardening is not like project managing. If I was filling in a time sheet for what I did this afternoon it wouldn't be very productive. 4 hours' weeding. Because so much of my garden sows itself, and that's what I want it to do, I have to weed all the time, ninety per cent of the self-sown plants being weeds. But I didn't go into the garden just to weed. I went into the garden because I love being there. Even if there were no weeds I'd still spend four hours late on a Sunday, after giving writing workshops all weekend, just being there. This is something no project manager would ever understand. Margery Fish would have. She did all the weeding at East Lambrook Manor by hand. She banned the hoe from all but the vegie garden because she couldn't bear to pull out a flower, by mistake, with the weeds. Christopher Lloyd wrote of his mother dead-heading the daffodils, '3 hundred and 45, 3 hundred and 46', out loud. He says he still counts when he's dead-heading. This isn't time management. It's love.

Dear Janice

I was out shifting lambs in the frost this morning. One hundred and one. One hundred and two . . . ! A bleak boiling grey cloud was slowly obliterating the sun. Between the froth of clouds an Air New Zealand jet was flying from Australia towards Christchurch. I thought, 'They don't know what's going on down amongst the rumpled folds of hills that disappear beneath the wings of the plane, those warm cosseted people. They're anticipating their arrival, gathering their duty-free purchases, retouching their make-up, and down below it's a black frost morning and I'm rounding up lambs for the works.'

Most mornings I like what I do. I feel smug walking the hills with the wind in my hair. I feel a wonderful freedom as all those people pass overhead trapped in a flying cylinder. I think of the flu-laden, recycled air tickling their nostrils, but this black frost morning I felt a tinge of regret that I was not one of them.

Henry has killed and eaten his third rabbit: Flopsy, Mopsy and Cottontail down, just clever Peter to go. Henry didn't catch the rabbit entirely on his own — I found it sheltering behind the pool filter and caught it in my hands, gave it a merciful dong on the head and gave it to him. He paraded the rabbit proudly around the garden before eating it for tea. The same night he bailed up a possum in the garage which I shot with the .22. Being rather partial to possum he ate a large portion of that as well. He came in later looking like a sausage that had swallowed a balloon.

I know how horrified you are at all the killing of little animals but it is a matter of protecting the garden from invasion. There is an old rabbit warren underneath the house in which new rabbits will set up house given the slightest encouragement, and as for possums, they strip the roses like a locust plague if we don't shoot on sight.

I have cyanide-baited feeders strategically placed around the outer reaches of the house, wool shed and yards. Between the feeders and the night shoots in the garden we would kill 100 possums a year. We estimate that over the entire farm we are grazing maybe 6000 possums who would all be delighted to move in, and they do as each vacancy is created. The battle is never won, which is why I'm ever vigilant at the ramparts. But not much longer: the exterminators from Target Pest are at hand.

Dear Virginia

Over my entire garden I could be grazing 6000 snails. They seem to love cold, wet weather. I suggest to them they'd all be happier in Tierra del Fuego. I don't bait them, or shoot them. But I do pick them off the undersides of leaves and — well, stamp on them. The birds applaud this like spectators in an Ancient Roman amphitheatre.

I did a lot of looking today, not aiming, just looking. I admired the self-sown seedlings, a carpet of finger-high cosmos, mixed with the delicate lobelias, everything so dainty, new, and all their own work. I merely weed. They do the rest. I looked at the amount of colour I have in the garden in the autumn. The deep red of the grape leaves on the garage are the high drama at present. There is bog sage, so blue, some viscaria from a late planting, polyanthus, white frilly cosmos, huge pink cosmos, nemesia which is so dainty and smells so sweet but which lies under the Complicata rose and needs a better address, and a view. Little heart's ease, pansies, white campion. A few roses on all the bushes, just one or two small blooms, here and there; diascia, lobelia. Those are small, delicate flowers, like pinpricks of colour in the air. The last hairy and huge nicotianas, one agapanthus flower, a beautifully rounded daisy bush with pale pink daisies on it. A few shasta daisies left. A bunch of vivid California poppies that shine orange in the sun.

In pots are splashes of red geranium, red globes of Hearts chillis, the cyclamen frothing with new leaves. I am still picking ripe tomatoes, from plants I've pulled out and hung over trellises and chairs. The feijoas are providing breakfast and snacks, and they perfume the kitchen. Polyanthus are flowering. The tamarillo tree is the highlight of the garden now and will be for a month. Its fruit hang like Christmas decorations. They aren't ripe yet, but show up dark red speckled with green. Bulbs are shooting upwards, but in general the garden feels as though it is resting in the warmth of a balmy autumn.

So a few hours just seeing all this, and weeding too. Quality time.

Tonight, I looked at my jeans leg because the dog and cat were staring at it. There was a pale, shaking stick insect climbing my leg. These little dinner-table dramas don't happen to non-gardeners.

Dear Janice

When I walk down to the dog kennels to feed my dogs at the end of the day, the whole garden glows. The sun throws a deep yellow light as it sinks behind the hills. The silver birch leaves are bright gold, the copper beech is burnished copper, and the huge yellow leaves of a magnificent weeping elm are falling slowly all day and the lawn is covered in a crinkly yellow and orange carpet. I will leave the leaves until they turn brown and soggy before I rake and mow that lawn. It looks so pretty. The perennial border on the other side of the drive has sprouted red and white spotted toadstools like fairy mushrooms. They are the most alluring of the fungi but also one of the most deadly, which is a shame. How exotic they would look in a green salad. The back lawn is sprouting toadstools, too, but they are the unglamorous brown and spongy variety, like old men's noses.

The vegetable garden has yielded the last of the summer vegetables. I picked green peas the other night and found a last potato with small white tubers. I've pulled up the cucumber vine and the zucchinis. The tomatoes are hanging on under their frost cloth and the tomatoes in pots on the terrace have ripened more fruits. These are another Kings Seed tomato, Oregon Spring. The catalogue notes say it is adapted to cool summer nights, setting parthenocarpic fruits (fruits can be set without pollination) when temperatures fall below 10°C. The flavour is intense and sweet. I think the tomatoes will continue to ripen for a little time yet. If they set below 10 maybe they'll ripen below zero. The air is colder this week.

In one of the garden cul-de-sacs there is a large holly tree underplanted with camellias and hellebores. The holly tree looks like a Christmas tree, it's decorated with bright scarlet berries. Blackbirds are eating the berries. The Christmas look is transient and by next week will have passed altogether, but it is magnificent while it lasts. I have picked some branches of holly berries and put them in the dining room and wished that they would last until the shortest day, but the berries will shrink into holly currants before then and the leaves will wither. The blackbirds will depart when they have eaten all the holly berries and be back when the pyracantha berries ripen. The fantails have flown as have the Welcome swallows, but the magpies are still, as always, quardle oodling in the branches and we have bellbirds visiting for the grevillia nectar.

It is a Thursday morning and I have postponed going outside so I can finish this letter. I should be out mustering cows on Lady, but most thankfully my brother-in-law Sandy is here from Sydney to do it instead. It is a prick of a day with strong, cold westerly gales. Sandy is not looking too excited about the day either. I will go out soon to shift sheep, in a nice warm vehicle and then I will vacuum the pool, which is strewn with autumn leaves, and I will mow the lawns, all except my autumn lawn.

Harry begins hunting tomorrow, on Batman. Batman is a new horse with a 'reputation'. He threw his last rider after jumping a fence, shattering the rider's leg painfully and badly. Harry bought Batman after the disillusioned rider decided he wasn't very fond of Batman any more. Now I'm in a panic because if Harry is smashed up I can't load the silage wagon to feed out. I can feed out if the wagon is already loaded but cannot load it myself, pathetic. I pray Harry doesn't crash out tomorrow, before I've mastered the silage business.

Dear Virginia

Help is at hand. I do know a little about feeding out. I have friends who have a lifestyle block up the coast. Last spring they were going on holiday. I house-sat, and bottle-fed pet lambs and FED OUT! This involved two paddocks, with steers in them. I had to move the steers from paddock one to paddock two, with Bunsen, masquerading as the intrepid cattle dog, turning his head into the wind so his ears blew back, crinkling up his eyes — he TRIED to look the part. He and I climbed to the top of the hill. There were the steers, like an ominous dark copse on top of the hill, and like a copse they stood still. They did not move. Vainly I flapped my arms around. (I guess I should have been equipped with a mustering stick.) Bunsen sat down to lick his legs clean of mud. Then one steer swung his head back and forth, stepped forward, and charged. At me!

I turned and ran. As you must know, running down a hill that has sheep tracks crossing it is very difficult, especially in gumboots that belong to someone with bigger feet than you have. I was running as fast as I could, but Bunsen the fat Lab was fair flying over the ground, ears straight back, eyes bulging. I heard a terrible high howl. It was Bunsen crackling through the electric fence at the bottom of the hill. It took me an hour to retrieve him from under a flax bush — having to walk all the way round the electric fence and coax and drag the terrified dog home. He spent the rest of the day cleaning himself and reading the paper. I phoned a farmer up the road. He came round and completed the muster, with a stick to wave, and a very loud voice.

The other steers to be fed were in the bottom paddock. I was to give them a bale of hay (or whatever it was) twice a day. To do this I drove the Capri sports car down to the hay shed, manhandled a bale into the boot which was exactly big enough for one bale, then drove (with top down and boot up) to the steers' paddock which was alongside the road, hopped out of the convertible (bright red one), heaved the bale over the fence, jumped back into the car, did a Uey and returned home for a shower, rest, drink, and a good book.

June

Dear Janice

1st June, now that winter has officially begun you will have moved on from your hunter-gatherer foraging for compost. I laughed about you visiting your friends armed with bags so you could gather leaves for your compost bins. I do not need anyone's leaves. Autumn leaves tumble from the trees and form a dense carpet which has to be raked into huge piles and redistributed around the garden. I use most of the leaves for mulching the flower borders. I do not make 'official' compost as you do, but I do have compost bins. My bins are made from posts and boards and are wide enough to allow the tractor forks in to turn the compost. My compost doesn't heat in the same way yours does as it is an on-going process. All year I add all the weeds, lawn clippings, dry cuttings, spent plants and leaves to the pile, every now and then I sprinkle a bit of lime onto it. I don't buy lime in little bags from a shop as you do, I get it 'off the back of a truck'. I shovel a bit into a barrow from the lime truck when it is here spreading lime by the ton. After a year and a couple of turnings by tractor, the compost pile has compacted and turned into crumbly earth which I use in my flower pots.

P.S. I read Mandy your letter about feeding out in the sports car: I'm sure she thinks you're mad. What is happening to your garden in June?

Dear Virginia

I don't know what is happening in my garden in June because it's dark when I leave in the morning, and dark when I return in the evening. Every day is counted — to the shortest day and then from the shortest day, waiting for longer days, so that I might catch a glimpse of the garden again at the beginning or end of a working day.

In the weekend I noticed honesty plants springing up from where last year's one plant was. Honeywort is similarly colonizing a whole triangle. Silverbeet and tatsoi forests gleam at me. They looked crayoned rather than real. There are also daisies, and still some cosmos. Felicia, which is a blue daisy that I'm very fond of, is flowering in the mail-shed bed. The camellia sasanqua has its perfect creamy pink blossoms with the fold of cone-shaped petals in the centre. And the garden's altar, the tree tomato tree, looks so Byzantine in the richness of its colours. The fruit are deep, deep red, heavily hanging, swinging in the breeze, bigger even than Christine Rankin's earrings. They glow in the winter garden like lanterns in a Christmas tree. What tropical luxuriance in a Wellington garden in June.

Dear Janice

I have a very yummy recipe for pickled tree tomatoes. They go well with lamb or cheese or you can just eat them whole if you are a pickle sort of person.

Spiced Tree Tomatoes (or Tamarillos)

2 kg tree tomatoes
500 g white sugar
250 g brown sugar
2 cups white vinegar
1 cup water
6 cloves
1 piece of root ginger, sliced
1 cinnamon quill

Skin the tree tomatoes by covering with boiling
water. Put all the other ingredients in a saucepan
and bring to the boil. Simmer for about 15 minutes
and then add the peeled tree tomatoes, simmer
for another 5 minutes or so. Remove the pot from
the heat and carefully spoon the fruit into warmed
jars. Pour the hot syrup over the fruit and cover.
Leave for a couple of weeks before eating.

I love ginger, so when I make this recipe I use a large piece of
ginger, but it's up to you. Recipes are like road maps — you
don't have to follow the main route, I like taking side roads,
sometimes you end at a completely unexpected destination.

Winter has begun. We are into the feeding out and break
feeding regime. But the feeding out has just been revolutionized
with the purchase of a new tractor, a second-hand John Deere
tractor. John Deeres are green and yellow tractors; next time
you go driving in the country take note of tractors. You will see
that there are many green and yellow ones. Our new tractor is
small by most standards but is bigger and smarter than our old
one. It has a dinky little clutch lever that you can work by hand,

lots of gears and ratios, a tinted glass cab, air conditioning and central heating, a stereo and CD player. The tractor is a dream to drive, so smooth and so quiet, it doesn't sound or feel like a tractor at all. Harry now comes in at lunch time and tells me who was on National Radio. I don't hear any world news if I'm changing the hogget breaks, and feel uninformed.

Henry is in his element, lolling about in front of the fire most days.

Dear Virginia

Instead of a new tractor complete with National Radio, my most indispensable tool is a hand-held piece of bent wire used to weed the beds. It has a plastic-covered handle but is still a rip-off at $4. I also have a spade, to dig out agapanthus, secateurs, and a broom to sweep the paths, those paths I increasingly do not like. In spite of this tool, the garden today looks a weed-filled mess. And the shape is all wrong. Triangle beds are too angular. I fear a complete make-over mood is coming on me. Restlessness and dissatisfaction are characteristics of gardeners whose plots are too small and whose ideas are too big, when winter is near.

This is what I do to tree tomatoes. It means I can eat breakfasts in the cold pre-dawn on a working day, when each spoonful is a lake of summer. Once a week, in the magic of the weekend, I pick one ice cream container full of tree tomatoes. Inside again, I pour boiling water over them in a big bowl. After a while I peel off the skins. I slice the fruit into a large jar. I add a tbspn of sugar and leave them. The next morning they are soft, dark red, saturated in a deep ruby juice, ready to spoon into a bowl with yoghurt, porridge, cereal or whatever.

Good morning, Janice

On a chill winter's morning, three degrees at 11.30 a.m. I think you should know what has been happening on your farm in North Canterbury.

On June 4th, Harry mustered in the cows for pregnancy testing while I began pruning the raspberries. Ken Fraser of Fraser Scanning arrived at one o'clock with his assistant Jackie and his fifty thousand dollar scanning machine. When we first began pregnancy testing cows the process took most of a day. Each cow had to be crushed. This is not as dreadful as it sounds. In our cattle yards there is a narrow race forward of the drafting gates. The race exit is controlled by a two-sided metal gate arrangement with a sort of big key-hole in the middle. The gate is called a cattle crush. The cow walks towards the open crush gates. At the precise moment her head passes through the key-hole bit the operator pulls a heavy ratchet lever down and the metal wings clang shut about the cow's neck, holding her in place for the vet to do his thing. The vet's thing in those days was to determine pregnancy by plunging a gloved hand and forearm into the cow's rectum to enable him to feel the foetus. If you can imagine this invasive procedure you will understand why some cows kicked, snorted and bellowed. Pregnancy testing was a lengthy, boring and sometimes hazardous business.

Ken's machine consists of a device that reminds me of a hand-held post office tower with a revolving restaurant on top. It's a steel probe with a rotating scanner that transmits the picture of uterus and foetus or lack thereof to a tiny screen in the visor of Ken's helmet. The helmet is a sinister headpiece, black, a cross between an upturned bucket and a motorbike helmet. If Ken had taken breath stertorously you might have thought Darth Vader had descended upon the yards. The probe still detects the foetus via the rectum but the cows don't seem to notice the intrusion. There was no need to crush them. We filled the race five cows at a time. Ken tested each cow in a trice and we were finished within two hours. The pregnant cows began the trek out to Rollet's gully that afternoon. The unlucky dry cows await a rise in the beef schedule and transportation to the works. Infertility is inexcusable on a farm. Fecundity is the only way to survive.

I always have a sense of foreboding when we are pregnancy testing. We were pregnancy testing the day the Cave Creek platform fell. The 28th April 1995 was a cold southerly day on the Canterbury side of the main divide. Mike the vet arrived at nine and we worked all morning in the rain; there was mud, crush clanging, sloppy cow dung and a wet wind with a mean bite. At 12 o'clock I left Mike and Harry bantering about nuclear ship visits and walked back to the house to prepare lunch, de-mud myself and don city clothes to attend the 'meet the teacher' afternoon at Fleur's school in Christchurch. At 12.30 I drove out the gate in the rain. At school I chatted with friends and met with Fleur's teachers. My friends asked after Kit, I told them he had 'found his own space' at the Tai Poutini Polytech on his Outdoor Recreation course. He was blissfully happy, I said.

On the way home Fleur and I stopped at the Tea Bahn in Leithfield to buy a satay pie for her and a coffee for me. As the man behind the counter poured the coffee he said, 'Terrible about the accident at Punakaiki, wasn't it?' A whole crowd of people had fallen off a platform, he said. We hadn't heard the news all day so I asked questions. It was like playing one of those elimination party games where you are the last person left standing without a chair. The man offered me his telephone, I rang home but Harry didn't know any more than he'd heard on the radio and TV. The police wouldn't release information to anyone over the telephone. It was after six o'clock at night; Harry hadn't heard from Kit but neither had we been contacted by the police. He was faintly hopeful. The café owner obviously wasn't. He wouldn't take any money for the coffee. A small girl in the café handed me a bunch of flowers. I felt a fraud, I wasn't a grieving mother, Kit was alive.

But I wasn't a fraud. The platform fell at 11.30, Kit died an hour later; about the time I left for the city. How could such chaos be happening on a blue sunny day on the other side of the mountains at the end of the road? I always believed a mother would know if a child was in pain. There were no signs that morning, no forebodings, only the slow plodding cows, the clanging of the crush, the stinking mud and the stinging rain.

* * *

Your garden has got away; yes, bring in the garden tidiers. They may even bring a tip-truck, a small environmentally sensitive one, to carry away the debris. The difficulties start when they say 'So you want to change your paths, Janice? And shift the vegetable garden? Now where exactly would you like us to shift them to?' And you don't know because in actual fact you need a landscape architect like they have in those garden make-over programmes. I hope Bunsen will be consulted too, about the re-siting of his en suite.

Dear Virginia

There is no pregnancy testing in my garden. The only crusher is me, pushing stems, prickles, thorns &c into the compost bins.

A few days ago, mid June, I had spaghetti with the last of my own sautéed red cherry tomatoes. The basil died or was all used up quite a while ago, but the tomatoes, after the big clean-up, have been hanging over the trellis around the garden gate. The leaves have withered and dried and the tomatoes have remained plump, and have gradually turned red. They are delicious. So that is six months of tomatoes from my tiny garden — and I have jars of tomato soup still in the freezer to eat even later in the year.

For that last spaghetti I swirled olive oil in the pan, with garlic then added the tomatoes, rolled them to coat each with oil, cooked till the insides were soft, added chopped chives and parsley and the very last basil, and piled it all into a bowl with pasta. On top, to give it the extra oomph food needs in the dark winter days, I grated Parmesan cheese. Perfect.

Dear Janice

June 18th — Yesterday morning Harry went hunting, the tally-ho sort. I had the farm to myself along with a list of instructions. My dogs and I drove first to the swamp paddock to shift the steer calves on to a new break in the green feed oats. It was a morning after frost, the swampy earth ice hard, the sky bright winter blue with a white diaphanous half moon, left over from the night, slowly sinking behind the hills. The air was so clean it smelt of nothing at all but cold and silence. A plover shrieked at our coming, flew up, shrieked some more and flew away. The sound of silence resumed. It was a perfect morning.

The garden is sleepy in June, not much is happening so I will tell you about bull sales. June is bull sale month on the farming calendar. That is the time when farmers buy new bulls for the mating season. We like to have three Aberdeen Angus bulls, two Hereford bulls and four Charolais bulls on the farm. Some years we attend two or three bull sales, but this year we only needed a Charolais bull which we bought at the Silverstream sale for $8500. His name is Silverstream Tudor, I shall call him Tudor Rose.

Attending bull sales is a ritual that has changed little in the thirty years we have been farming. Most bull sales are held on farms and the bulls are auctioned by the stock and station agencies. After the sale the vendors put on a barbecue with beef steak sandwiches, beer, wine, coffee, tea and savouries. If you were a retired farmer you could amuse yourself attending bull sales and being generously wined and dined. The Te Mania bull sale provides one of the best feasts. The Wildings cut juicy slices of meat from a huge rolled beef spit roast and serve them with bread and salad and mussels fresh from the sea at Kaikoura.

I'll take you through a bull sale. The catalogue arrives weeks before the sale. This allows you to study the form. Each bull's breeding, parents and grandparents, is catalogued, along with his weight, recorded in this case on May 7th; the weight per day average growth rate is calculated, his eye muscle area, rump fat, rib fat and scrotal circumference measurements are listed. To pre-empt your 'what's scrotal circumference got to do with it?' — scrotal circumference is an indication of a bull's capacity for semen production. In the middle of the catalogue there is a table containing the Estimated Breeding Values of each bull. The EBV system is a nationally ranked classification of an animal's estimated genetic merits, including ease of calving, milk production, 200-, 400- and 600-day weight gain, carcase configuration, and more. You evaluate all this information and select the bulls you like on their genetic potential and estimated performance credentials. On the day of the sale you must spend time looking at the bulls in the flesh.

Bull sales are a ritual; the auctioneer takes the podium with his cohorts representing the stock firms at his side; on the ground a phalanx of agents stands scrutinizing the crowd for bids. Bull sales are a male domain. The auctioneers and the stock agents are all men. Most of the buyers are men. They particularly do not expect women to be bidding. A few years ago I was deputized to buy a black bull at the Culverden bull sale. When my chosen bull entered the arena I lifted my catalogue in the discreet manner I'd seen Harry employ. No one took my bid. I lifted it with more deliberation, still nothing, and then I waved the bloody thing in the air. Fred Fowler was auctioneering. He looked out across the bull ring with surprise, 'Are you bidding, Virginia? Oh, I'm sorry — the bid's here with Virginia.' My cover was blown. There is a convention that you bid very discreetly so rival bidders do not know who they are bidding against, hence the discreet dip of the head, the doff of a cap, the drop of a finger.

The women's movement has made few inroads into the Stock and Station agencies. I've heard of female stock agents but never seen one. One afternoon when an agent was sitting at our table having a cup of tea after a stock valuation, I teased him about the all-male preserve, saying that one day women would make advances into the inner sanctum. He vowed that this invasion just couldn't take place.

'Why not?'

'Well,' he blustered and flustered, 'well, it's hard dirty work, long hours, time away from home, and well we couldn't talk the same. We couldn't tell jokes and stuff.'

'But, come on, women can do all those things,' I said.

'Yes I know, but it just wouldn't be the same and it'll be over my bloody dead body.'

I do not know how the firms have maintained their all-male preserves under the Equal Employment Opportunities legislation. Maybe they recruit female agents then slowly strangle them with paternalism and dirty jokes.

Tell me something funny in your next letter.

Dear Virginia

I attend lots of book launches, my equivalent of your bull sales. But the soggy vol au vents can't compete with your rolled beef spit roasts, and scrotal circumference is never even considered when selecting a celebrity to launch the book. As for EBNs at home here, it was a mere distant dream of Bunsen's that he had any scrotal circumference at all.

This weekend, through a veil of rain, I saw lots of birds in the garden — fantails, blackbirds, thrush, sparrows, greenfinches, chaffinches, waxeyes. There are a few solitary roses — Dublin

Bay never stops. Graham Thomas is still golden. There's jasmine. I picked it for a vase, but few of the jasmine pink buds opened into their white stars to perfume the house. I guess I was too early, and the house is too cold when I'm at work.

Dear Janice

Saturday, 15th June — I have to write. It's snowing and the garden is dusted with white frosting. For me falling snow never loses its fascination. Even though we have suffered all of snow's most disastrous consequences I still love watching the flakes float down. The hills are white, barely distinguishable from the white sky. The deodars are snow-frosted like Christmas trees. The silver birch branches and twigs are encrusted with snow, and beneath the birch the rhododendrons are bowing and bending, burdened by the flakes caught in their leaves. I am going to be forced outside to knock the snow off before all the shrubs are permanently deformed. It is hard to believe, but if shrubs are left weighted down with snow for more than a day they never fully return to their former shape. We had some very snowy years in the early 'nineties which permanently reshaped many of the evergreen shrubs.

Is it winter in the city? Winter is when my letters will be delivered in a plaintive wail. I rail all winter against its short harsh days and long nights. You'd think we live in the frozen tundra the way I lament my climatic exile. Growing up on the East Coast ill-prepared you and me for harsh winds, snow, frosts, ice and long dark nights. Even Wellington must seem a cold, windy, damp place after Turihaua beach.

Today I have been pruning New Dawn back to bare stems. She trails over an archway in the vegetable garden and has become so dense this season that she is shading the carrots and my three surviving parsnip plants very seriously. It is not the optimum time to prune roses, I know, but New Dawn is such a triffid sort of a rose that I don't believe this will stop her growing just as rampantly next summer. There are piles and piles of prickly runners all over the bricked part of the kitchen garden and I've ordered the tip-truck again.

Poor parsnips. I think I told you in an earlier letter that something dug up most of the seeds and ate them. Yesterday I had to pull all the leek plants out as they were afflicted by a kind of mildew. It is the same one which affects onion plants and I think it might be called white root rot or maybe it is downy mildew. It is very disappointing. Garlic, onions and leeks have always been trouble-free crops until last year when I noticed onions turning yellow. When I pulled them I found the roots shrivelled and rotting. Now it's the leeks. I shall have to spell the garden, no more leeks, onions or garlic for a while.

It seems that more and more plants, once trouble-free, are succumbing to newly introduced pests and diseases. Some are old diseases which I've by luck managed to avoid, and others new arrivals to NZ like the gooseberry mould. We used to grow beautiful gooseberries and a few years ago this devastating mould arrived. Harry got down on his knees and gave thanks for the arrival of the gooseberry mould, whilst I sadly ripped out all the plants and burned them.

The end result of the onion mould is that we have no leeks for the winter and are left with only carrots, three parsnips, one silverbeet plant (you remember the wandering pig ate the winter silverbeet) and eight Brussels sprouts stalks. In these days of supermarkets and greengrocers the crop failure is not serious, but it makes you realize that in the pioneering days such a failure would mean a bleak and uninteresting winter diet, or worse, starvation.

As it is we will have a bleak and uninteresting winter diet because I shall feel morally obliged to eat all the Brussels sprouts. I cannot understand why the pig didn't eat them. I seem to remember Gub Gub, Dr. Doolittle's pig, was fixated on sprouts. Self-seeded rocket is springing from bare patches where the mesclun mix grew. It is not frost-sensitive. The coriander is frost-tolerant, but I have it under plastic because it looks feathery and fragile. There are a row each of inedible cauliflower and broccoli and celery. The broccoli has been deep-frozen twice and is looking ugly. The celery has turned transparent. I will keep you posted on the cauliflowers. The last lettuces have been deep frozen. As you might expect, this does not suit them, they turn brown and slimy as they thaw.

I must go now. It is actually tomorrow from when I started writing this. The ground has thawed and warmed, the sun is shining and Harry wants me to shift some errant cattle and the hoggets.

Dear Virginia

I too have plant disasters. Last year I had Iceland poppies flowering at this time. Not this year. I think it is because blackbirds have been particularly exploratory and destructive amongst the mulch and the soil. They kick and peck the mulch out of the way and dig into the soil in their search for worms, and toss out any poor plant that's in the way.

I am dreaming of . . . a tall garden, like Giverny. In a Monet print on the wall everything is tall. The planting is orderly, standard roses with beds of red geraniums behind them. I dream of space to do big plantings of just two plants together, like this.

Do you want to hear something funny? I overheard two suited male bureaucrats yesterday. One was telling the other about his new job. 'The archiving is excellent. There's a veritable suppository of information,' he said.

Dear Janice

Farmers are often laughed at for being slow so I loved the story of your office workers; no one but a slow moron could have 'a veritable suppository of information' at his finger tips.

We went to see a production of William Congreve's *The Way of the World*, written in 1700. The country cousin was announced — Sir Rowland, knight of the realm no less. Guess what? He bumbled on stage, a belching boorish buffoon. Perceptions haven't changed much in three hundred years. We are still being portrayed as belonging to a doltish rural idiocy. Have you noticed that in most ads featuring farmers the farmers talk slowly? The implication being that if you talk slow the brain is slow.

There is a schism between the city world and the country world. I become a different person when I cross the gap. One day I am wearing jeans, jersey, gumboots and Swanndri, sloshing around in mud, talking with dogs, and the next I'm coiffed, made up and drinking cappuccinos in the Arts Centre or even strolling Lambton Quay dressed in the obligatory 'capital city black', meeting people like you and Fleur for lunch and hopefully not looking like a city person's image of a farmer. I'm not ashamed to be a farmer but goodness me there seems to be something amusing about looking like one. The rural woman is an object of mirth. Sometimes when shopping an assistant, making conversation, will ask me what I do. I say, 'I'm a farmer,' and she will say, 'Oh, but you don't look like a farmer' and I say, 'What do you think farmers look like?' and she giggles, 'Oh, well, sort of red-faced, fat and wearing a woolly jumper.' Intellectuals must think farmers occupy some other world too. Wordsmith Max Cryer once said on his radio slot that farmers wouldn't know the meaning of 'short black', 'clearway' or 'infill housing' but that they would know what a swingletree was! I wondered who was living in the real world that morning. I had to go and pour myself a short black and look up 'swingletree' in the Oxford dictionary.

Anyway, I was thinking about all this as we were riding home in the moonlight with a mob of cows and the light from a lime-yellow half moon began to cast dark tree shadows across the grass. We live a life that is part of the New Zealand mythology: horses, dogs, sheep, cows. Once it was part of the New Zealand dream.

Hill-country farming looks romantic to city people and sometimes it is, as it was tonight, as we clip clopped along the laneway in the dusk, slouching beneath a warm hat, the horses steaming and the sweet musky smell of the sweat rising into the cold space around my face, black cows sloping ahead in the gloom, and afterwards leading the horses down to the stables, brushing them down by the light of a single electric bulb swinging naked from the roof, pouring oat chaff and sweet feed into the feed stalls, the horses munching and snorting. Moments touched by nostalgia even as we live them, but life on the farm is not always so sweet. I must tell Janice that, I thought, in case she thinks farming is all moonlight and steaming horses. I must remind her that sometimes farming is cold and dirty, boring.

Farming is like playing Monopoly: every year you complete a circuit of the board. It's a closed circuit, round and round the board with seasonal regularity. Some years the seasons are kind, other years they are not. Once a year you pass Go. In the providential years you collect the two hundred dollars for passing Go; in the bad years you don't, you borrow from the bank.

July

Dear Janice

Today is the first of July. July is such an untrustworthy month for farm and garden. Most years it passes with benign indifference and then, a rogue year, and it turns upon us in a savage cold fury of icy rage. In 1992, the year of the 'big snow', the farm was blanketed in snow for ten days. Harry and I spent long frozen days snow raking. Snow raking has nothing to do with rakes. It is the term used for rescuing sheep imprisoned in snow camps high in the hills and shepherding them down to feed and water. While we were snow raking, the poor garden, crushed under a mantle of frozen snow, had to fend for itself. The grevillias and camellias never recovered their shape, and the privet hedge lurched about the garden in drunken disarray for several years. Hundreds of birds died.

Another July the world froze over. Night after night the frosts fell from a cold starry sky until the sun could no longer unfreeze the days. The ice grew out from the banks of the river until it met in the middle and I could stand on it and watch the bubbles flowing beneath my feet. The flaxes and cabbage trees in the southern barricade withered and died of frostbite. Out in the gullies great swathes of flax perished along with ancient cabbage trees and manuka bushes. My nephews and I sawed round holes in the swimming pool ice pretending to be Eskimo fisherman. There were no fish. The vegetable garden became an ice concrete wasteland and the carrots and parsnips couldn't be chipped from the earth. And then the sky unfroze and the water pipes burst into gushing fountains and geysers.

We hope for a better July this year.

Dear Virginia

I rarely get a frost, tucked under the hill, but we get endless dampness. Rain, mist, wind. But no snow. We've just had another wet weekend! This time a southerly with rain squalls. Walking as fast as I can home from work, in heels, the rain slaps me about, each slap leaving that sparkle of shock that causes me to gasp. This is ugly winter. This is the moment when spring seems very far away indeed. This is the moment to turn round, rush into the travel agent's, and book a horizontal hot holiday lying on a beach. But no! The money is for a pergola, paths, plans. And I really am not a horizontal holiday person. Have faith. I cling to the motorway overbridge's railings as a gust knocks my bag against me and nearly bowls me. I struggle on.

As soon as I reach home I take Bunsen for a walk. I dress in gear that Shackleton's men would have thought excessive. I wear a merino singlet, polyprop top, polar fleece jersey with high neck. I have polar fleece pants, thick woollen socks. I pull a woollen hat onto my head. Then a parka and scarf form the outer shell. Bunsen wears his winter collar, which is made of slightly thicker plastic than his summer one. He doesn't notice changes in weather. A walk is a walk regardless.

We go to Wilton's Bush, a small (74 hectares) valley of original and regenerating rimu, matai, kahikatea, miro, hinau and northern rata bush between Northland and Wadestown, 5 minutes' drive from my house. At the edge of the bush, I catch the shock slash of silver as a silver fern is whipped by the wind and shows the underside of her wings. Water rages down the normally gentle Karori Stream. As soon as we enter the bush we leave inclemency behind. Here it is almost still. The wind whips through the tree tops but we are far below, one of us marvelling at the leaves all around us, varnished to a high gloss by the rain, the other sniffing a tree trunk, checking for p-mails.

Dear Janice

I loved reading of you walking in the storm with Bunsen wearing his winter collar. My dogs are neglected. They do not have winter collars and when I take them walking they are working. One afternoon at the end of July we were out, my dogs and I, mustering a block we call the Peninsula and I wondered how I could convey the exhilaration of the moment to anyone who has not stood on top of a hill, alone in the late afternoon with the sky yellow to the west and the wind howling through the bowed tussocks like the sound track on a David Lean movie. We were chasing the last of the hill ewes out of the Peninsula through a gate at the bottom of the block. At the top of the highest peak on the block I made the mistake of looking back. A good musterer never looks back, an old-timer told me that. And 'bugger', I saw five sheep. I ran Muffin wide to head the sheep off. She caught them just at the moment they believed they had got away, she stood poised, one paw in the air eyeballing the sheep. They stared back, they held their ground. Muffin is not a strong pulling dog. I sent Toby out to break the impasse and crossed my fingers, toes and eyes. Toby is a Blue Beardie, Blue Beardies can execute brilliant manoeuvres or they can wreck a muster. Toby was having a good day. Toby and Muffin pulled the ewes round the side of the hill towards Tan and me. They passed below on a sheep track running into the wind and away towards the west. I called the dogs in. We stood on the high peak, to the four points of the compass I could see no sign of human habitation, just brown hills to the north, the south, the east, and to the west the high foothills rising rugged and blue-hued to the mountains, snow-draped against a wild grey and yellow streaked sky with navy clouds boiling over the ragged tops, and all the time the wind buffeting and plucking at the matagouri and the tussocks and me, blasting around the rocks on and on and I wanted to scream and scream with the sheer joy of being there. And then at the corner of my eye a movement far below on the Milo track, a four-wheel motorbike crawled along, so far away it looked like a child's toy. Clem Small, the ferreter with his traps and his GPS wending his way homewards. I didn't scream. He wouldn't have heard me if I had — I couldn't hear his motorbike — but somehow the magic had gone.

I have an old friend, Pat, he's in his eighties now; I remember him telling me of times on the tops when he felt as if he were on the verge of a major discovery, almost as if the secret of life could be unravelled if only he concentrated hard enough. I feel it too, every time I stand atop a pile of rocks on the edge of a scream.

Dear Virginia

For weeks the wind sweeps curtains of rain across the pine-clad Tinakori Hill. The roar echoing off the hill doesn't stop. Bunsen and I used to stand on the top of that hill, look out at the harbour, and feel a little of the exhilaration you describe.

He's too old now to get to the hill top. I hunker down with him at home. I can't prune roses or grapes in this weather. I can't weed. Time to read the gardening books again.

Dear Janice

Last Wednesday we saddled the horses after lunch and rode up the road with all the dogs. We met John Rutherford, or at least he met us and had to slow down to first gear. He wound down the window of his Land Rover, jerked his thumb back up the road and said, 'The back country's that way'. We rode on up the Virginia road towards where the sun sets and mustered the paddock sheep down from North Virginia. They will not graze the hills again. They begin lambing in the paddocks in mid September and will leave Double Tops in January.

The Virginia blocks were named long before I arrived at Double Tops. They were named because they bounder the Virginia road. The Virginia road leads to the Virginia country, so named because it was virgin land. That is what I've been told and it is as good an explanation as any.

When the ewes were mustered to the northern corner of North Virginia, I opened the gate and Harry carefully shepherded the mob of ewes onto the road. They trotted down the road towards the paddocks and — then they all came back again — with my young dog Pixie proudly stalking the rear. There was shouting from the head musterer about 'people who cannot control their dogs', and vitriolic shouting in return. You always hope that in these work-related disputes the neighbours aren't lurking in the tussocks listening to every word.

On a still day the sound carries for miles, it is possible to be quoted, weeks or years later, over a dinner table conversation. Oh, the mortification. Even though the landscape appears empty, there is no guarantee you are alone. There are neighbours, weed inspectors, ferreters, pig hunters, trampers, tree pruners — any of these people could be abroad at any time.

One morning early I walked down to the wool shed to ask Harry what I was to do for the day. He was on his horse. People on horseback always look arrogant when you are on the ground and Harry said from his great height, 'Well, you can open the gate for me for a start.' I told him what he could do with his gate. 'You arrogant **###@ *&#@! Open your own fucking gate!' 'Oh well, if you want to make a scene,' Harry said sweetly and reasonably, 'you just go ahead.' I thought, that's funny, he's showing a lot of restraint, and turned around to find the Target Pest possum eradication team standing in front of the shearers' quarters listening to my tempestuous outburst.

Dear Virginia

I have neighbours, cheek by jowl with me. But because we are all at work during the day, and our cottages are on separate lanes, I rarely see them and we never have dinners together. Town is less friendly than country, I'm thinking. One night my sister-in-law stepped round her car to get into the driver's seat, farewelling me over the top of the car at the same time. She didn't notice the edge of the steep two-storeyed-high bank, and plunged down it. I managed to get her up. She'd been caught in tree branches. She was too shocked to drive home, and her keys were lost forever down the bank. Next morning she called a tow-truck to take her car home. No neighbours remarked on the bizarre goings-on at the cottage between the lanes.

A student who stayed with us for a while lost her key and came in through the cat door.

'Easy,' she said. 'We do it all the time in Germany.'

And still no neighbour queried someone dismantling the cat door and squeezing through.

Dear Janice

I'm reminded of another onlooker incident. I don't think I have introduced you to Terry, a shearer who works here sometimes when there is not much shearing on. He is also a Territorial soldier and another of our regular pig shooters. When he is here he mostly drives around in the white fencing Niva, the Terrymobile, fixing fences. We nick-named Terry 'The Terryfier' because a few years ago he renovated the boundary fence between ourselves and Melrose. The fence line was overgrown with matagouri and other woody weeds, Terry tore into the scrub as if it were the Timorese jungle, completely subdued it and rebuilt the fence. He did a wonderful job. Now whenever we have a difficult fence line Harry says 'Must get The Terryfier on to it.'

The other reason for the soubriquet stems from the time Terry and his assistant walked through the Veilchenblau arch to find me sitting on the bench at the back door drinking coffee with no clothes on. I had just had a swim when Harry handed me a coffee, I sat down to drink it in the sun. It seemed a safe thing to do because Henry always barks when strangers enter the garden. This day Henry did not bark. He loves Terry. So, there I was, a crinkled old lady, naked, sipping coffee and suddenly there was Terry saying, 'Oooh, dear, don't look, Ash,' as he put his hands over his eyes and peered through the gaps between his fingers. I've been 'terryfied' to skinny dip without a towel on hand ever since.

Now, back to the garden. It's time to tidy the flax border. I planted natives along the southern garden boundary because nothing else would grow. The house was built on the edge of a bog, waterlogged in the winter from the hillside run-off, dried to concrete in the summer by the nor'wester. What grew there before the land was broken in? Flax, cabbage trees, tussock, matagouri and reeds. I put them back, minus the matagouri, and added lancewoods, griselinia and matipos. The griselinia and matipo died one very wet year, and even bog-hardy natives carry no guarantee of survival: the ice winter I told you about froze the flaxes and cabbage trees. The cabbage trees resurrected themselves sprouting new spears but the flaxes died and had to be replanted. Once you own a cabbage tree you need never buy another. They seed everywhere; they like popping up amongst the driveway stones best. Have you ever lived with a cabbage tree? They drop dead spears all the time, it is unwise to mow them, the fibres are so strong they strangle the lawn mower rotor.

I'm not a 'natives purist'. I grow catmint and the orange-hued testacea tussock in front of the flax. I love blue flowers and the catmint links the flax with the flowering part of the garden rather than isolating it as a 'nativery'.

Dear Virginia

Yes, I have lived with a cabbage tree. It's a point of honour that, wherever I live, it will be with a cabbage tree. I planted a two-inch-high one (yoghurt pot, 5c from Robert's school fair years ago) in Karori, which was large when we left that house. The new owners chopped it down. I couldn't believe it. Here I planted one (this time $9 from The Warehouse) by the mail shed at the bottom of the drive. The mail shed is beside an old boundary wall. There's enough space for a person to squeeze between the mail shed and the wall — but no reason for you to do this, except that one day I discovered a strange man (strange in behaviour as well as a total stranger) squeezing between the wall and the mail shed.

I broke up old concrete in front of the mail shed (to make a garden and because I was furious) and piled the old concrete in the gap between the wall and the shed, then I planted my Warehouse cabbage tree in front of the pile. There! That'll tell people this is a no-go area. After a year the tree was growing well and then one day it was pushed over — obviously by another squeezer. I have no idea who these people are and why they need to squeeze round behind my shed which leads them to my steep bank. I mean, if they want to nosey around they could walk up the drive. I've propped the cabbage up but it doesn't look very happy.

I am about to go downstairs to make dinner for Robert and his girlfriend who are visiting for the weekend. They are in town to play pool at a pub in Courteney Place, meeting a friend of Robert's who is also a helicopter pilot and who has just had his first helicopter accident and been stood down for a few weeks. They arrived at 3 a.m., in Robert's 1960s' Valiant — an ideal vehicle for fencing on Double Tops? — which does not fit up my drive. They were late because they ran out of petrol on Highway One somewhere south of Taihape!

Dear Janice

Lucky you, you will be able to fly with Robert. I love helicopters. Most years we spread liquid fertilizer by helicopter. My big treat is to go for a fly around with Harry and the pilot to show the pilot where to apply the fertilizer. I love sitting in the ridiculously fragile-looking plastic bubble, the rotors winding up to a scream, I'm entranced when the ground suddenly tilts away beneath my feet. Lift-off is always a magical experience. The novelty of helicopter flight has never worn thin.

The funniest flight around the farm I ever had happened one cold windy afternoon in late autumn when TV3 rang to say that the Conservation Minister Denis Marshall had belatedly resigned from his portfolio. They wanted a comment from Harry and if he was available they would send a helicopter right away so the interview would make the six o'clock news, was Harry available? 'Yes,' I said with great authority. 'Harry is down at the sheds working on the tractor.'

When I went down to the sheds I found it was one of those days Harry had decided, on the spur of the moment, to do something else. I was still looking for him when the helicopter landed in the front paddock. It was a big bright-pink helicopter.

The pilot, who had flown seed and fertilizer here years before, suggested we might as well go and look for Harry so I climbed into the front seat beside him, put the earphones on, and off we flew along the Virginia road and then inland along the boundary track. We spotted a mob of merinos being worked by a dog long before we saw Harry. Meanwhile down on the ground Harry was muttering about deer poachers from the Coast becoming daylight robbers. He looked up to see a bright-pink helicopter with *Garden City Helicopters* emblazoned on the side.

Harry waved us down; we hovered and bucked about in the wind a while before we landed on a flat part of the track. The TV interviewer was wearing a little black number and unsuitable shoes. The wind was cold off the mountain snow. Harry was so surprised at the arrival of a pink helicopter into the middle of his muster, he had trouble responding in depth to the resignation of Denis Marshall. After the interview Harry flew off in the helicopter with the TV crew and left me on the ground to drive the dogs and the Land Rover home. I'm sure Harry's comments with regard to the resignation did not warrant the cost of the helicopter, but the scenic shots of the tussocks bending to the wind in the late afternoon sun were stunning.

We do not have any human squeezers or lurkers. The only lurkers in our garden are animals, the wild and the domestic variety. Garden lurkers come by night. If the back garden gate is open the horses sometimes amble up the drive and graze on the lawn. Sometimes they decide to walk straight through the garden along the drive. When you wake in the dark to hear the crunch crunch of a slow-walking horse on the gravel it is creepy until you realize it is only a horse. If my dogs start barking late at night I briefly wonder about sinister lurkers, but there is always a rational reason: a bitch in season, Henry midnight-prowling, the full moon. One warm summer night when I had left all the doors open I woke to a frightful din; I found my demented dachshund bouncing on the living room sofa and a terrified possum clinging to the top of the curtains.

Has your cat-door molester tried molesting again? Now that is much more scary.

Dear Virginia

I have told Bunsen to do guard duty at the cat door. He looks at me and his eyes say, 'Me? A guard dog? Who are you kidding?'

The soil is saturated and cold. Blackbirds ransack the garden ruins daily. They kick the pine cone mulch around, dig in the soil and send poppy plants flying. Every evening, when I come home, I see, with the help of the outside lights, the paths strewn with bits of plants, mulch, soil. Most can be swept back onto the beds but the poppies are goners. Now I realize why the English like box edging for their garden beds. Box would be back-stops for the birds' kicking practice, and they'd give seedlings some protection from the wind. Why are blackbirds so rapacious in the winter? Maybe they are very short of food and are digging deep for worms. Maybe the worms are coming up from flooded burrows, and in this sodden state are irresistible to blackbirds. Maybe the garden isn't as full of plants as it usually is and so birds can get down and dirty in the soil, having a dirt bath. I do not know. I love blackbirds for their beauty. They are the most elegant birds in my garden. I love the way they flick their tails. I love their deep blackness and their song. BUT I wish they'd take a winter break.

Dear Janice

Blackbirds, do not speak to me of blackbirds! Rapacious birds — no, that is too charitable a description. They are voracious, vexatious, vandalizing, vitriolic varmints and I love them and I hate them, our relationship is dichotomous. I watched, this morning, a convention of blackbirds conferring on the lawn — after voting and reaching a unanimous decision they all hopped over the edge of the grass into the vegetable garden. They don't scratch. They shift all that mulch and litter and soil with their beaks, they put their beaks into the mulch and they give their heads a tweak, whereupon a disproportionately large amount of debris is flung hither and thither. We know a meticulous man who tends a meticulous rhododendron garden, mulched to clipped lawn edges; he was driven to such a state of distraction by litter-shifting blackbirds that he covered all his mulched earth with chicken netting. The less meticulous of us just have to keep sweeping our paths and grinding our teeth.

You remember the unfortunate parsnip crop? I discovered the cause of the crop failure after I planted my broad beans (long after Anzac Day, regrettably). I hoed blood and bone into the seed line and then planted the beans. Next morning, from the kitchen window, I could see the pink-coated seeds lying unearthed and scattered. I went out and replanted them. Next morning, same scenario, the earth works were so major I decided it must be Henry digging for the blood and bone. But the culprit was not poor blameless Henry. It was a blackbird — there it was, beak in the dirt, shifting mountains of soil and pecking at morsels of pulverized blood and bone. I replanted for the third time and covered the dirt with a double layer of bird net.

I have another blackbird who has taken exception to the primroses. He has pecked off all the flowers in his territory. For all their bad habits I still like blackbirds, they are attractive birds with their deep black plumage and bright yellow beaks. They don't sing as well as the thrushes. Now the bellbirds; they are the divas of the garden. Their morning song wakes me at dawn. Each note is so perfectly clear you can assign a word to it and make the bellbird sing whatever you wish it to, over and over, a mantra for the morning.

Dear Virginia

I agree with you that blackbirds are the great trench warfare exponents of the garden BUT I love them. So — I plant most of my seeds in my In trays and transplant when they aren't seeds, AND I put upturned cut-in-half plastic bottles over the top for the first week too. It's tough being a blackbird in my garden. All they get is mulch and dog hair to line their nests.

I must prune the repeat-flowering roses, and grapes. I must check the passionfruit to see whether it has survived the cold and wet. I must mow the tiny lawn/en suite which is rough as pasture, and I must plant garlic. But I have only the weekends, and it always seems to be raining, or just clingy mist, or else I am away. This winter I haven't had many days of winter sunshine among the plants.

What's blooming right now? A few poppies — the ones not ripped apart by the birds. There's one Albéric Barbier rose out. The centre was deep cream when it unfurled. (Albéric grows over the motorway banks opposite the house. It's in full flower there in November, with centranthus and rosemary.) There's Graham Thomas of course — he never stops flowering. One Sparrieshoop. An Iceberg struggles up the fence and is surrounded by jasmine from over the fence. Daphne is out. Splashes of bright yellow polyanthus. Pansies — not enough to colour the ground, but one or two. And the ones in pots have large flowers and have to be dead-headed regularly. The camellia in the pot is still flowering, still more pink than green. But the rain has browned the blooms, which then fall in soggy messes. There's a blossom on the viburnum I bought last month. I think it will be a success, with its yellow jasmine climbing round it. Some viscaria is flowering delicately in a pot. Another pot of viscaria is not flowering. Such is the mystery of gardening. The felicia in the mail-shed bed, which I cut back hard in the autumn, has flowered all winter long, clear blue flowers.

The fruit is all finished, except for the last of the tamarillos dangling and glowing through frost and storm, like Grace Darling's lantern. Lemons are ripening.

Did you know 'Paradeisos' is Greek for 'garden'?

My thoughts turn to greens, to eat with roasts and gravies. Tatsoi is the best green to grow for the designer potager look. Each leaf is pristine, shining, and perfectly spaced around the centre. No insects chew on it. The plant is like a flat green rosette lying on the surface of the soil. So long as you space them well (about a foot between each one) you have perfect neat and tidy circles in your vegie plot. Mine are crowded together in one plot so they are a bit smaller than they can be. But one solitary one is surrounded by a ruff of variegated honesty (self-sown) that sets it off perfectly. If I was to go into a Rosemary Verey fantasy now, I could imagine a garden of tatsoi in rows with winter lettuces, or parsley, or even pansies, filling the gaps between the circles.

We are also eating silverbeet (red and white), spinach, parsley. It is enough to get us through this dark month.

Dear Janice

It is a month since I looked out the window and saw the snow falling. The grevillias and camellias sprang back to their former dimensions but the wretched privet hedge looks as though it has been trimmed by the drunkard again and needs major reshaping. You tend to imagine that not a lot happens in the winter garden but if you pause and look closely you see that things 'round the elm tree bole are in tiny leaf!' The grape hyacinths are springing. When we were together at Gisborne Girls' High School studying the English poets I could never understand 'Oh to be in England now that April's there', nor understand Miss Bagley's enthusiasm for the unfathomable elm tree bole, crocuses and hosts of golden daffodils. You could, but then you were born in England. Now that I live in a southern garden which goes to sleep for the winter I wait and watch with all the enthusiasm of the old English poets for the awakening of spring which announces the beginning of another year in the garden.

A number of my tiniest spring treasures have died, swamped and submerged by their aggressive neighbours, like the hellebores which are unwrapping themselves in every bed in the garden. In another month the hellebores will be in full bloom. I read that I should be cutting off the side stalks now so that the stems bearing the flowers stand unencumbered by last year's foliage. I like to leave the leaves on because they lie flat and suppress the weeds, but then on the other hand the beauty of the flowers might be enhanced if they emerge naked from the earth. Hellebores are beautiful in an understated 'beige' sort of way. They are one of my favourite flowers because they bloom when little else will. They are my winter roses.

My delicate crocuses have been suffocated, but daffodil buds and the hard folded points of the tulip leaves are poking out of the leaf mould. The first primroses, creamy yellow, are flowering under the camellias where the frost can't maul them. I must not forget to mention the winter-blooming ericas, they are in full bloom like snowballs. There are not enough ericas to make a difference to the winter aspect, I should buy some more.

I think this is enough for one letter. We are dutifully munching through the Brussels sprouts. But before I go I must tell you about the frogs. I was removing a large purple flax plant piece by piece from where it wasn't wanted. Deep in the sticky decaying centre of the leaves I disturbed two small sleeping frogs camouflaged in the rotting mass to a deep maroon. I held them in the palm of my hand just looking, loathe to release them, they were so perfectly beautiful.

Dear Virginia

I have plundered the Tasman Bay Rose Catalogue and Kings Seed Catalogue, for imaginary gardens. Kings Seed Catalogue is full-colour, with clear typography, easy to find your way around, full of tips and, of course, full of unusual plants. How do I deal with the cornucopia of it? I either have to go out and buy a large allotment, or cull my list of must-haves down somewhat. This is what I do. I check last year's seed packets and discover quite a lot of unused seed. I cross these species off my long order list. I go through the catalogue again and ruthlessly discard any plant that looks as though it's not ideal for my circumstances. I cut out any that have germination practices so complicated they are like rituals — nick one end, refrigerate for 10 weeks, soak for 24 hours before planting into soil onto which you have poured boiling water — then I print my list onto the order form, *then* I add up the prices. Never add up the prices before you print your list onto the one and only order form.

I have a more mystical approach to the rose catalogue. There are few photos. You have to go by the 2-line descriptions. The catalogue is organized by type of rose. I look only in the Climbers and Old Garden Roses. These usually are named after people, e.g. Cécile Brünner, or Mme Isaac Pereire. The names have more charm than modern roses called Glowing Cushion or Dimples or Big Daddy. Should I choose Great Maiden's Blush because that was the rose in Margery Fish's garden, when she moved to Lambrook Manor? Library books are scattered over the floor for the winter months, with Post-Its stuck out the sides. An evening to mull over such questions as — will it be Albertine or will it be François Juranville? The two lines of words about each rose are read and reread, to unlock their secrets.

Far far too many roses are on the initial list — enough to cover the Botanic Garden's rose garden as well as my little place. What to do? A new pergola is planned. An architect summoned. Drawings are done. A builder gives a huge quote. In the early morning — about 3 a.m. — I suddenly realize the pergola post will be coming through the deck. Fine. But there will be no soil under the pergola anywhere. A hole will have to be cut in the deck. Architects and builders don't really understand the basics of rose pergolas. Soil will have to be got from somewhere. And what's under that deck anyway? I suspect it's old concrete. Drainage will have to be sorted out. The builder says 'No sweat' and adds zeros to the quote. The gas fireside dreams about old roses continue. More books are consulted. That big yellow rose at Sissinghurst that Vita swears by, Lawrence Johnson, will be far too big. My little plot is not Sissinghurst. Cross it off.

July is full of dreams of what could be, full of longings to scatter seed, to nurture seedlings, full of images of snorkelling Pacific lagoons, full of other people's holiday photos, full of rest on the couch before the onslaught that is spring.

What did you do with those frogs?

August

Dear Janice

Were you worried about the purple frogs? I love frogs. They are not furry. I warmed them in the palm of my hand so they would have enough energy to find a new hiding place in another flax bush, then I let them go.

August is the beginning of the end of winter. The grass tries to grow and there are fecund flappings in the bird community. The hapless pied oystercatchers have returned to build another 'nest with a view' in the middle of the laneway. I call them hapless because they always incubate their eggs on unsatisfactory sites and never raise any chicks. The paradise ducks are squabbling in the trees and around the sheds. Paradise ducks often perch in trees. It seems wrong, a water bird perched in a tree. They're savage creatures and sometimes fight each other to death. The male blackbirds and thrushes are pirouetting about the garden in aggressive mating dances and the first unplanned lambs are born. The lambing should not begin until September but there are always promiscuous sheep who jump the fence.

It's 'odd job' time. We always think we are going to get lots of odd jobs done in August because it is an uneventful month. We never do get the odd jobs done: they go back on the list for next year. Odd jobs are house and garden maintenance, hedges, sheds and pathways. All women living on farms complain about the lack of priority given to 'odd jobs'. There are trees I want sawn down, a new vegetable garden fence. The vegetable garden fence has been on the list for five years and the trees awaiting felling cast more shade every year. Harry finished building me a wonderful raspberry frame three years ago; it was five years in the building!

Harry does not have a lot of spare time. Down in the workshop is a whiteboard on which I write lists of jobs to be done in the garden. These are jobs requiring heavy machinery or chainsaws. I know I should have learned how to use all these implements of destruction myself but I'm not Super Woman. Harry sometimes finds there is a spare afternoon. He informs me, at lunch time, that work in the garden will commence after lunch. I have to think very quickly, there is no room for indecision. Indecision is time. A chainsaw is a very final implement: 'Quick, where do you want the branch off?' Brrrrm, the branch is lying on the ground and I'm thinking: now did I really want that much off?

Most August mornings are absorbed in feeding out and break fence shifting. These jobs are essential farm house-keeping like feeding the family and vacuuming the carpet, prudent but boring. I know that you know all about feeding out — in sports cars — so will spare you another description. You may not have done break feeding; break feeding is a feed conservation tool. A paddock is rationed out daily, each morning a new strip of fresh grass or green feed is fenced off with a temporary electric fence. This is the break. Shifting break fences involves pulling out reels of electric tape and hooking it through plastic fence standards. If you are not good at logistics you end up walking the fence line many times making adjustments. You can also shock yourself if you are a careless person. A 5000 volt jolt is uncomfortable. It thumps your heart and it will throw you to the ground if the fence 'knee taps' you on wet mornings.

Some people are not discombobulated by shocks. Terry, the fence terryfier, thinks electric shocks are healthy. 'You need a shock once a month,' he declares. The other employee who didn't mind shocks was Russell. Russell was a very cheerful young man from England who worked with us over one winter. I have a funny story about Russell. One day Kevin Rowe, our stock agent, was here drafting late lambs and lamenting the fact that the Hawarden 'marrieds' rugby team was short of players for the annual marrieds versus singles match. Russell offered to play for the team. 'Played a bit of rugby, have you?' asked Kevin. 'Yeah a bit, but I haven't got any gear with me,' said Russell. Kevin found Russell some gear and on the day of the match the captain put Russell on the wing out of the way. We heard that no one passed him the ball in the first half. The locals were a bit dubious about a strange pom. 'Could have been just some useless wanker,' someone said. What Russell hadn't told anyone was that his 'bit of rugby' included playing for the England under-nineteen team and that he could also run a speedy hundred metres. When one of the marrieds team did pass him the ball the opposition were left standing in the mud. Russell took many passes after that and the marrieds won the game. Russell was amused but very modest about his contribution to the win. We were sorry to see Russell leave.

At the start of August the man from Mainland Minerals called to discuss the fertilizer requirements for the spring. I asked him if Mainland Minerals did garden packs of fertilizer. 'Oh yes,' he said. 'We can do a soil analysis for you and make recommendations as to your fertilizer requirement.' An elementary soil analysis cost $60 dollars which I just slipped onto the main fertilizer bill. The report arrived last week in a smart blue folder. It read, *V Pawsey — Area analysed — Vege Garden*. The summary read, *Performance of your soil at 'Vege Garden' will improve markedly if you address the following requirement — Sodium levels should be increased.*

The report recommended that sodium chloride (salt) be applied to the garden at the rate of 2.5 gram per square metre. The report says my garden has an excellent cation exchange capacity; that means there is an excellent capacity to store calcium, magnesium, potassium, sodium and nitrogen. The soil pH should be allowed to fall to achieve optimum conditions for availability of mineral elements and plant growth. Sulphate levels are in excess and the available phosphorus is in excess. The man from Mainland said that if pasture levels of phosphorus were that high he would be worried about sheep eating the grass. 'The phosphorus will be leaching the calcium out of your bones,' he said. I immediately felt fragile about my hips, drew my spine up straight and vowed to drink more milk. No more layers of sheep manure for a while and no more side dressings of Nitrophoska Blue. The report goes on for *another 15 pages* about trace elements and worms, humus, anions, lime, calcium.

We get very detailed reports for our farm soils. We employ a strategic approach to fertilizer application rather than chucking tons of superphosphate and nitrogen all over the farm. We like to encourage soil biological activity and earthworms so we use a liquid limeflo fine-particle fertilizer. Some farmers think we are mad: 'Might as well piss into the wind,' one farmer said, but we are very pleased with the results, and hell — we get to ride in the helicopter twice a year.

Dear Virginia

I have not analysed my soil. Maybe I should. In the good olde days to test whether soil was warm enough for seeds a man would do a down trou and sit his naked butt on the soil. If the soil was too cold for comfort, it was too early to plant seeds. I read that somewhere. Winter forces me to read far too many impractical gardening books.

All I can tell you is that everything that comes out of my garden is returned to it. And the mulching moments provide it with extra desserts in the form of seaweed, pine needles, leaves, and dog hair. The soil is crumbly, soft, dark. If you push a 6-feet-long bamboo stake into the soil it just goes down and down and down. No clay. No bedrock. The early settlers grew potatoes along this warm, sheltered flat area. And Ron, my neighbour in the next terrace, still grows them today — a whole city section of them. It seems the least I can do is protect and nurture the soil.

Books tell me winter is the time for devising new garden schemes, planning new plantings. But no, it isn't. Winter garden dreams are too fanciful to result in workable plans. They just lead to trouble. It's wet, cold and dark out there. I've almost forgotten what the garden actually looks like. I make lists of seeds and roses I think I need — hundreds of them. I do mental gardening. I plan sweeping driveways lined with agapanthus and cabbage trees. I twine clematis and honeysuckle through the netting of a tennis court. I think of armillary spheres . . .

Totally out of control, I hired a landscape woman who drew a plan that wasn't ever going to be my garden. She saw the garden as a thing to look at. I see it basically as a thing to eat. They are different visions.

Virginia's urgent email

The trouble with today's landscape gardeners is they do not appreciate the vegetable because they are not of an apocalyptic frame of mind nor have they been through a war. They cannot imagine a time when you might not be able to pop down to the supermarket for a pottle of mesclun mix, an aubergine and a cucumber.

Dear Virginia

Too late! I hired her. The landscaper presented me with a beautifully drawn plan, softly coloured in pastels. My concrete cross-over paths were changed into gravel ones in a square-sided 'C' with one side open to the deck. The deck was cut down in size without the silly built-in seats. The middle of the new, central rectangle would be a lawn. So the garden would be more open, the lawn a breathing space in the middle. Very nice, I thought. But where do the roses go? And the carrots?

Tradespeople come and go, shake their heads, offer different variations.

'Ah, you want all the concrete paths taken up, do you? And gravel laid? That's a lot of work.'

I respond by modifying the plan. The landscaper gets upset that her proportions and her vision are being tampered with. I agree with the builder: there are concrete paths there already. Just break them up and re-lay them. 'No!' the landscaper says, with, it has to be said, a smirk: 'That would be ugly, and the paths would be too narrow.'

'But the width they are has served me fine. They don't need to be wider.'

'Yes,' she says very bossily, 'they do.'

I decide not to point out to her that Emily Whaley, formidable southern matron and gardener of Charleston, Virginia, wrote: 'The important thing is to keep paths narrow in a town garden. Mine are no more than 20 inches wide.'

Then I wake up in the night realizing I am not happy with gravel paths bordered by wood (to keep the gravel in), because bare feet on gravel when hurrying to move the hose in the summer to get in a quick watering of something precious before work, or running to the washing line to grab the clothes when it starts to rain — impossible!

The landscaper and I talked.

I said, 'In summer you can't run out to pick some herb or vegie barefoot, not on gravel.'

She said she knew a place where I could buy nice French plastic slip-on garden shoes.

I said, 'In the weekends I weed fiercely and throw the weeds on the path to toast in the sun before sweeping them all up for the compost. That wouldn't work with gravel.'

She looked around, at my paths strewn with dried weeds, and sighed.

I said, 'Gravel requires weed mat, I don't want to grow weed mat. And, worse, tanalized timber edges. I don't feel comfortable with arsenic leaching into the vegie garden.'

But we're talking 'looks' here, not soil health, her eyes conveyed.

I said, 'Bunsen's turds would be hard to remove from gravel.'

She didn't have an answer to that one.

So, in the end, I chose good old concrete. Nice and warm on the feet in summer, easily swept, and no weeds are going to poke through. Meanwhile, the garden sits there, untended. The landscaper and I have marked out the paths with string. I have cleared all the plants away from these new pathways, including a straight row of tatsoi. Now I wait for people capable of smashing up concrete and rearranging it, and chopping metres off my deck. They must be out there somewhere.

Dear Janice

We are still munching through the Brussels sprouts. Chef Lois Daish to the rescue — we tried her puréed sprouts with butter, cream and mustard, an improvement on bare sprouts though they looked suspiciously like the puréed vegetables my children refused to eat when they were babies, not a good look. I've not been fond of sprouts since the winter I worked in Norway. We ate boiled fish or sausage, boiled potatoes and boiled sprouts every night until I thought I would never eat another as long as I lived.

We still have carrots and rocket and side shoots on the broccoli. The coriander is proving to be as tough as old boots. I'm hoping it will be like the chervil which I planted years ago. I let the chervil seed, it migrated all over the garden and lodged behind the privet hedge underneath the shelter trees where it grows like an aromatic shag-pile carpet.

My winter roses, the hellebores, are resplendent. I know you have to look at them upside down but their centres are exquisite, especially the deep magenta flowers. Flower arrangers complain that cut hellebores wilt but you can use the flowers for arrangements if you either run a very fine skewer up the middle of the stem or otherwise split the stem up as far as the first bifurcation. The flowers don't wilt — but they still seem to drop stamens all over the table.

Dear Virginia

Another wet weekend. Nature obviously doesn't admire an office worker who can be outdoors only in the weekends. I put on my parka and garden regardless.

The only space in the garden now is up in the air so we've built the pergola for my roses. And the Tasman Bay order has arrived. François Juranville is planted against its pole. I hope it scrambles and blooms, and droops and does all the things I imagine for it. It better. It has the place of honour on the pergola.

Albertine is by the back porch. I know you warned me she will spread like plague but Margery Fish said she would always pick Albertine and put her into bowls in bedrooms in her manor house. Mme Alfred Carrière will ramp (a Vita verb) up the mail shed. At present she sits like three dead spikes, beside the mail shed. She likes sun. She'll get it. She's meant to grow huge ('vigorous' is what the catalogues say). That suits me fine because the mail shed could do with a hat of blowsy roses. August Gervais is planted next to the passionfruit on the wall beside Bunsen's lawn/en suite. Lest you think this is a crumbling, sun-soaked ancient brick wall, I will explain it is a corrugated iron wall, and rusting. The idea is that August Gervais will hurl himself into the arms of the miro tree and drape himself there. Along another corrugated iron wall is Veilchenblau. I know not to drink coffee under it when naked. It won't get any sun at all until it starts to 'ramp'. Will it know effort will greatly improve its outlook? Or will it feel sorry for itself and give up?

Mme Isaac Periere is also in the shade, along the side of the garage. Will she fling herself outwards and upwards towards the sun? I hope so. I chose her for her scent which is always described as 'heavy'. Choosing and planting roses is all about fantasy, hope, and reading between the lines in rose catalogues.

Now back down to earth. I have weeded. That chickweed, duckweed, whatever it is, is everywhere! I get more each year. I blame Bunsen. He must bring its seed home on his coat. August is the time I reclaim my poppies, stocks, nepeta, stachys, nemesia, honesty, polyanthus, foxglove seedlings, pansies and sweet peas from drowning in the green sea of weeds. Some plants, like the sweet peas, can't be extricated from it and have to be composted. Others, like the poppies, can be, but I have to be careful not to get too near that central root of the poppy and loosen the plant slightly in the soil. Any wind would then just spin the plant round and it would die of dizziness or take flight like a frisbee.

A ray of light. This morning, after rain, the sun shone through the silver birches about 8 a.m. The whole trees, leaves, twigs, stems, trunk, seemed made of silver. It was wonderful, especially with a matte blackbird flicking through it.

Camellias aren't my favourite garden plants. They become thick with dark shiny leaves, letting through little light, blocking sun. They are heavy in the landscape. I prefer plants that move, that let light filter through. Camellias do flower, which is nice. But most of the time there are flowers and dead flowers all on the same tree. The dead ones look like brown sodden tissues. When they eventually fall *plosh* onto the ground they look even worse. If you tread in one, it slimes on the path like dog poo.

However, my camellia, in its pot, is 7 feet high now. I prune it after flowering, so it has long wavy limbs and plenty of air in the tree. When it's not flowering I put it in a corner of the deck, in the shade, for the summer. When it's in flower very few other things are, so it gets moved to the middle of the deck. All this mobility is possible thanks to plastic pots. Very large plastic pots are a boon. You can act like an Ironman and roll, wheel, or carry your tree around the garden, a feat impossible if your tree was tethered in terracotta.

It is Friday night. I am waiting for Saturday, when I can burst out of the house and into the garden I last saw six days ago! My Kings order has arrived. I've bought the seed raising mix. I have some sand. I have trays. I intend to plant seeds and tuck them under the porch for protection. Too early, but why not? Take a risk. Hope.

Dear Janice

Yes, take a risk, they are only seeds, it's not as if lives are at stake. Well, I hope not. Do seeds know they are alive? It's too early for me to risk sowing seeds, even in seed boxes. Speaking of seeds, our autumn-sown paddocks are overrun with orphaned piglets. They are massacring the fine new grass shoots. The piglets live in the gorse beside the paddock and stroll out to graze when the sun warms the day. Piglets are adorable, but they grow into aggressive bristly pigs. I had a piglet named Clair once; she used to be able to tell the time. If ever I was late with her meals she would squeeze through the back fence and knock on the kitchen door with her nose. One afternoon when we had city guests there was a knock on the door, without thinking I got up and opened it. In charged Clair. All the guests screamed as she skated round and round the table squealing and grunting and bunting her nose into people's legs. Poor Clair, she grew into a bossy bristly pig and we shot her after she ate Olivia the pet lamb. We know she ate Olivia because she left Olivia's skin, with four little black hooves attached, lying on the grass.

Maybe I *should* try sowing some seeds. I could put them in the oven on fan bake to simulate the spring.

Dear Virginia and piglets

This is what I do when I sow seeds:

> I put my seed packets in a pile, sorting them like cards. The ones at the top are the ones that can be planted in seed trays in August indoors.

> Then I arrange an assembly line. You can do this on a bench in the garage or shed. I do it on my kitchen bench, after I've cleared away all crockery and food. The important

thing is that it's not on the ground. Crouching for an hour isn't so much fun.

I spread newspaper over the bench.

I bring in a plastic bag of seed raising mix.

On the left on the bench I place a tile and my coffee stirrers (wooden sticks you get with take-away coffee from coffee carts on Lambton Quay or The Terrace). I break each stick in half, except for one. I leave one unbroken.

Next to them I place my indelible marker pen, then the scissors then the container full of paper clips. Then the seed catalogue, then two In trays. I've never understood why my In trays at work have drainage holes but it makes them ideal as seed trays.

It's satisfying to fill an In tray with compost. (I usually select the third In tray down, the one where minutes of meetings and memos about new policies have been sitting for months.)

I line each In tray with the old memos, which have been well soaked.

I place each one in, or on, an oven tray to catch the drips.

I fill the trays with seed raising mix. I smooth it down, pressing it into the corners.

I firm it down with the tile.

I pour water over the soil. Not too much.

I pick up the unbroken coffee stirrer and make a line across the soil with it; a little furrow.

I pick up the pen and write the name of the first packet of seeds on one half of a broken coffee stirrer.

I cut the top off the packet, taking care that the name of the seeds isn't cut off too.

If the seeds are dusty-tiny, like lobelia or poppies, I pour them into my hand and then shake them into the furrow.

I check the seed catalogue to see if the seeds need light to germinate. Lots do, like salvia. If they do I shake them beside the furrow, rather than deep inside it.

Some seeds need 6 weeks in the fridge first, to trick them into believing they've had a winter. Those seeds I put into the fridge, after writing 'fridge' and today's date on the packet.

On my calendar right now I have written on 28 September's square, 'remove bleeding heart from fridge'. People may wonder . . .

I never use all the seeds in the packet all at once.

I fold the now-open seed packet up, so the name is clearly visible, and close it with two paper clips from the office's stationery order.

I repeat the process with another seed packet. And another.

For each packet of seeds, I make a furrow, like stripes, across the seed tray. One furrow for each type of seed. One named coffee stick at the end of each row to identify them. 5–7 rows in each tray.

I stack the In trays one above the other, just like in the office.

I put the stack inside a roasting pan, or a cat litter tray, to catch the drips. A cat litter tray works well. You don't need a cat. You can buy the trays at the supermarket. (I now use cat litter trays at work for In trays because they are bigger and deeper than standard issue In trays and hence suit my workload better.)

Then I put the trays on a table near a sunny window.
Then I do nothing at all.
They do the rest.

Today I planted: salvia turkestan, poppies, red flax, rocket, bronze mignonette lettuce, Mexican mint, campanula bellflowers, cornflowers, annual hollyhocks, baby blue eyes, lobelia, Virginia stocks.

I will have plenty of plants to give away!

It's best to stick to the simple seeds. Forget the tacca black bat plant that requires temperatures of 30 degrees plus bottom heat plus between 30 and 270 days for the seed to germinate.

Good news! I have finally got a builder person to come and do my new paths — so I will have a lawn in the centre and new paths. He's starting on Monday. I will let you know what progress happens.

Your writing to me about the events around Kit's death has helped me make the decision to visit Boyd's grave in London. Robert was three when we buried him and we've never been back. Thirty years and still too painful. We'll go in late September, and we'll take a silver fern from Wilton's Bush.

September

Dear Janice

It is eleven o'clock at night on the first day of spring. Harry is away fighting a fire on Double Tops. I have folded the washing, vacuumed the carpets, almost solved the *Listener* crosswords. I am alone. Outside the window the night is black. I'm waiting for the phone to ring, listening to the wind, waiting for Harry to drive up the drive, worrying. I hate these times, I hate the nor'west wind in spring. You cannot trust it. I feel very alone, waiting, not knowing what is happening.

Spring is the burning season in the hill country. Balmy spring afternoons are stained with smoke from burnt hills. Burning is permitted between July and the end of September but only with the prior approval of the Regional Council. We apply for permits and after the burning season has ended inspectors fly over the farm to check that we have not exceeded our brief.

Some farmers burn sections of the farm every year as a matter of policy. We don't burn a lot and the burners cannot understand our wilderness approach. When they visit you can almost see their itchy match fingers twisting in their pockets. 'Needs a bloody match,' they whisper to each other. Harry once gave a paper on the 'Do Nothing' approach to matagouri control at a seminar at Lincoln College. Harry was an advocate of the Do Nothing approach for a long time, but the matagouri flourished with such zeal we were forced into burning as a control measure. A farm is like a perennial garden. If you can imagine a perennial garden that is never dead-headed or cut back, the lawns never mowed, the trees not pruned — it would become matted and unproductive, and it would be a fire hazard. Now do you see the need for a burn once in a while? To burn matagouri we let it grow for ten to fifteen years, until it is tall and thick. We shut the block to cattle for a season to allow an understorey to grow and on a sunny, warm 'zephyr' afternoon we torch it.

Harry looked out the window this morning and declared it a burning day; warm, light winds forecast, dying down in the evening. And why is he still out at eleven o'clock at night? The fire got away. He was burning Mandy's Face (named after Mandy, it's a sunny face). The fire was very hot. High flames leapt the fire break track and bolted up the face. The winds did not die down as forecast. They are rattling the windows. Harry and Andrew grabbed a pie for tea and departed armed with shovels and wet sacks and a cell phone. I'm here to answer the phone and call for reinforcements if they are required. I hate fires when they do not behave.

I was going to say 'I hate fires' full stop but that would be a lie. Fires are seductive. Almost everyone is a secret pyromaniac given a free hand with matches. You light a clump of dry grass with one match, grab a handful of tussock, light it from the first flames then run seeding fire in to the undergrowth. As the fire feeds on itself the flames explode into skyscraper plumes of flame, burning red, orange, yellow, in an orgy of choking, crackling heat, and the smoke spirals hundreds of feet into a mushroom cloud of smutty brown before the wind disperses it to a streaky stain in the clear blue sky. The association of mushroom clouds and nuclear destruction is unavoidable.

I look at the devastation after the flames have died, the crumpled grass smoking into fragile piles of ash, and the charred branches of the matagouri bushes, scorched stones and the blackened earth, and I wonder how many geckos fried, how many birds died. I feel ashamed of my demented flame throwing.

'Ah, but nature is cruel, death is part of life' another voice in my head says. 'There could have been a natural summer fire, a lightning strike in all that overgrown scrub and that would have been worse.' There is always this dilemma in farming, between economics and nature. We cannot farm productively if the whole farm is overgrown with scrub. We try very hard to balance economics and the natural environment. There is one block we will never burn, it is called The Matagouri Block. It's like a bird sanctuary. When I muster it, flocks of yellowhammers, waxeyes, grey warblers fly ahead of me in clouds. The block does not yield much grazing, but it does provide shelter in a storm. Every time I struggle through the thorns and bush lawyer searching for sheep and losing sight of the dogs I curse its wilderness and would gladly take to it with a flame thrower, but then billows of birds fly up, they swirl, chirping and tweeting and then they flutter into the scrub ahead of me and I think, no, this must always be a preserve of the birds.

It's next morning . . . Harry and Andrew arrived in, red-eyed and stinking of smoke, about midnight. We sat around the kitchen table and drank a few beers. Harry joked that I did not need a beer because I had not been fighting the fire. I said that the stress of not fighting the fire, of sitting alone waiting beside the phone, was harder work than fighting the fire so I drank two cans of beer.

Back to describing yesterday, September the first. While Harry was lighting fires my dogs and I mustered the merino ewes from the Bush Block into Tommy's Creek. The Bush Block is a long rumpled ridge running from east to west between Tommy's Creek to the south and Cabin Stream to the north, the south face is scrubby and steep with a small stand of beech trees. We drove along the bottom of the south face along the Tommy's Creek track, hoping no sheep would be grazing there. But mustering stock never works out as easily as it could; we came upon fifty ewes munching grass on our side of the creek. A few deep barks from Tan and they took off along the river bank to the Lancewood Bush where they crossed the creek and began a steep climb all the way to the top of the ridge. I'm taking you on another muster because I was so proud of Toby. He shepherded the sheep up to the ridge like a pro.

The back of the Bush Block is a classic run Harry likes to reserve for his dogs; it's a huntaway challenge. I always itch to run my dogs up it. Watching Harry work a dog up the face is like watching Tom Sawyer paint his fence. While Toby shepherded the ewes, Tan, Muffin, Pixie and I sat on a tussock bank in the bright blue afternoon and watched. There are not many balmy bright blue days in the hills, so you make the most of them. You take it slow. A bright blue day is to be ambushed by joy, the hills are soaked in sunshine, the air is soft, skylarks beat trails in the sky. So I sat at peace and watched Toby creep behind the ewes as they wound their way between the rocks and bushes in single file like a wobbly string of pearls. Toby didn't bark. He climbed, he sat, he climbed and sat in a demonstration of patience and restraint until the ewes disappeared over the ridge.

Tan was intensely jealous and stood aquiver, watching Toby's every step, waiting to be sent out to assist. She can be a silly dog when she is excited and would have barked and overrun the sheep in her enthusiasm. When a dog is shepherding sheep up a hill there is a psychological tipping point. If the dog oversteps the point and runs too close to the mob, the sheep at the rear become uneasy. They turn and bolt down the hill. Young dogs and silly dogs bolt after them. In the wild a dog's instinct is to separate one sheep from the flock and kill it, so when the dog bolts it is responding to its instinct — shepherds override that primal instinct with training. Toby's instincts were under control throughout the climb. I was very proud of him.

Dear Virginia

Shortly after I'd moved in here some neighbours came to visit. Instead of bringing a bottle they brought a hub cap and a sheet of iron. They placed the iron on my deck, put the hub cap on top, then filled it with sticks and finally a couple of logs. Then, while I poured the chardonnay, the guy poured kerosene over the pile of wood and lit it. Whoosh! He spent the evening hypnotically feeding the fire with any old wood I had lying around.

Dear Janice

2nd of September, I got the maternity case ready. The maternity case is a blue plastic briefcase that once contained an animal health remedy. It is a robust case, ideal for carrying the lambing equipment and keeping it clean and dry. What is in a lambing briefcase? Bearing retainers, disinfectant, wash cloths, calcium borogluconate, syringes, and a lamb stomach tube feeder. I put the case and the lambing crook behind the seat in the truck.

What's a bearing retainer? A bearing retainer is used to

hold a bearing in place. I used one this morning. My heart sinks when I see a ewe with a pink balloon like a bubble gum ball bouncing at her rear end because it's a bearing and it must be seen to right away. The bearing is a prolapsed vagina which fills with urine and swells until it ruptures. The remedy: catch the ewe and tip her over on clean grass. Ideally you wash the bearing with an antiseptic wash then you gently manipulate and squeeze the pink balloon to allow the urine to escape. When the pink balloon has shrunk to a squishy lump you push it back in and hold it there with the retainer. The retainer is like a plastic coat-hanger with a shoe horn in the middle. The shoe horn bit goes inside the ewe to hold the vagina in place. The bearing usually wants to pop straight back out so you have to quickly tie the coat-hanger ends to the wool with tape. Getting the tension right is fiddly. Once parcelled securely you let the ewe go. She leaps up and runs away with a nice red plastic coat-hanger round her bottom. The retainer is pushed out of the way when the lamb is born and hopefully we get it back at tailing time.

Calcium borogluconate is used for treating ewes with milk fever. Milk fever is a chemical imbalance which can occur during late pregnancy, the ewe becomes weak and wobbly, eventually she lies down; left untreated she dies. A subcutaneous injection of calcium works miracles, arise-and-walk miracles. The old *New Zealand Farmers' Veterinary Guide* says that if calcium is unavailable it is possible to cure most cases by inflating the udder with a bicycle pump. The mind boggles. We do not own a bicycle pump. For my mountain bike tyres, I use the compressor with a bicycle pump attachment. It's a powerful and rapid inflating device with which one might unintentionally inflate the whole sheep.

Dear Virginia

What can I say? You make me feel so inadequate. I have never had cause to use a bearing retainer at the office. Massaging ruptured vaginas is not part of my job description.

The concrete paths were laid. Thank you, Claus. The landscaper returned to check the paths and posts. She suggested the paths were rather bright, white, and perhaps I'd like to colour them.

'No!' I roared.

She reckons the lawn should be next to the deck. I reckon the lawn should be girdled with a herb border — maybe thyme, then a row of small vegetables, then a row of roses, then lavender bushes, tall English ones, against the fence. She offers to come round and help 'move plants'. She sneaks a look at the huge turkestan salvias which I planted last year. They are smack in the middle of where she wants the lawn. I say no way. They didn't struggle for a year for presence in the garden — from their start in a Kings Seed Catalogue picture that grew in my mind, all the long journey to the vast rough-leaved plants they are now — to be dug up, huge roots and all, and dumped on the compost, in exchange for a sprinkling of lawn seed. No way.

Dear Janice

I do not need to employ a Mr Claus. I have the wonderful Harry who has a full range of implements of construction and deconstruction down in the tractor shed. Harry thinks that all parts of the garden should be accessible by tractor. He is not into intermediate technology like wheelbarrows and shovels.

Dear Virginia

This is the month when weeds grow faster than vegies, annuals or perennials. Whereas flowers are like words, planted carefully in lines across the page of the garden, weeds are like typos — there's always one you miss, and someone else seizes on with delight.

Zucchini seedlings don't need molly-coddling like your lambs. They just get on and do the business of transforming themselves from seeds to big, hairy, tough plants. They are perfect for children to plant. You just plant the seed in a pot. (I used a plastic container that had been full of marinated mussels. Zucchs aren't fussy.) Get on with your life for a week. Then a plastic-looking, smooth, shiny head thing, as large as a button, appears. Within one working day it's pushed the soil from its top, unbent, looked up. The thing that looks like the back of a head turns out to be the base of two powerful leaves that open and give the plant a big-mouthed Muppet look. I plant it out on a mound of rich soil and stand well back.

Dear Janice

18th September, it's a wild windy day with driving rain from the nor'west sweeping across the mountains. We are just on the edge of the storm in the horizontal rain belt, to the east the sun is shining and the sky is blue. Yesterday I was in Wellington being a city person, drinking espresso coffee, watching all your compatriots spilling from their offices at the end of the day. Today Harry and I are shifting break fences in the rain. The lambing conditions have been depressing. Too much nor'west rain. Imagine how it is for a newborn lamb. Take your Wellington gusty winds, lace them with sheets of heavy horizontal rain, shift them south, elevate them to 1500 feet plus, put on some thin clothing then go and stand outside all night in a roofless paddock. You would be dead in the morning. Lambs born in a rain-drenched gale do not survive. We have to be relaxed about it because there is not a lot we can do when all the sheep live in the hills.

We lamb the old sheep in the paddocks and we do look after them during storms. Sometimes during a difficult birth I play midwife. Most of the lambing difficulties are caused by the lamb not presenting correctly in the birth canal. When the lamb is born it should slip out head first with the two front legs forward beside its head. A common problem is for one leg or both legs to be left behind. If one leg is back you can sometimes crook a finger behind the lamb's knee and draw the leg forward, if there are no legs showing you might have to ease the head back in, rearrange the lamb and then pull it out. The worst scenario is when there are two back legs showing, a breech birth, or when the legs and the head appearing do not belong to the same lamb, that's two lambs trying to arrive together. The mixed arrivals are tricky. You have to squeeze everything back in and disentangle the bodies. It's like putting your hand blind into a bag of very warm water. You feel where the lambs are, make sure you are pulling one lamb and not two. You think, I'm never going to sort this. Your wrist gets squashed by the contractions. It hurts. Your hand loses strength. When at last you've pulled the lamb out it lies still a moment. You pull the placenta away from the mouth. The lamb shakes its head and takes its first breath, it's a special moment. After the birth you place the floppy, steaming lamb under the ewe's nose, rub some placenta round her mouth so she has the lamb's taste on her tongue and knows she has given birth. When she begins licking the lamb you can slowly ease away and leave mother and baby to bond.

So far this spring I've only assisted Sunshine, one of the fat pets. I found her lying down with a big swollen lamb's head poking out. The lamb's eyes were glazed with white film. It was very dead. The head was too swollen to push back in but there was enough room to squeeze my hand alongside the neck and find the two legs. I pulled the lamb out then explored the uterus for a sibling but there wasn't one. Sunshine didn't care. She didn't even look at the dead lamb. She just got to her feet and began eating grass. The resilience of sheep is astounding.

Dear Virginia

Nature's own terrorist, spring, has come to Wellington. Wind, storms, gusts, racing clouds, howling pines, roaring gullies, sea spume spitting at you, waves breaking over the coast road, tulips and magnolias battered in the Botanic Gardens. In my garden, more sheltered than most, the poppies fire salvos of orange flame across the newly cleared pathways-to-be, from bunkers hidden under the weeds.

Wellington's winter is often mild but spring is always violent. And every day, Monday to Friday, I have to struggle across the motorway bridge, holding my coat wrapped round me so I won't take flight like a land yacht. Gusts are the worst. You aren't prepared and suddenly it's on you, cutting your eyes, pulling your hair out, tugging at your clothes, knocking your work bag against your legs so the zip snags your tights. You arrive at work looking as though you've been in a battle, which you have.

I just keep weeding, pruning, and sowing seeds. In a storm, like the one that lasted all of last week, I snuggle in bed, thinking of the seeds. They don't worry about storms. Nor do they worry about me. But that force that makes them change shape, seek the light, grow and flower is a force I lack on a Saturday morning in a southerly gale. I turn over and go back to sleep.

Dear Janice

Last week we found a young cow with a foetid placenta dangling, a bad sign. Calving cows is more difficult than lambing ewes.

You use the same technique as you do for assisting sheep but everything is bigger and heavier. Pulling a lamb requires grunt. Pulling a calf requires a lot of grunt. Sometimes mechanical intervention is necessary. We are very gentle, not a bit like the 'bugger' ad which suggests the farmer may have pulled the cow in half with his Toyota. We aim to end the delivery with a live cow and a live calf.

We ran the cow down to the yard and into the cattle crush. Harry washed up then lubricated his arm and made an exploration. The calf was breech but presenting two hocks not two back hooves. He couldn't manipulate the calf at all. The vet was not available. The situation was hopeless. There was only one thing to be done, dog tucker. Harry shot the cow, skinned and gutted her, then we hoisted her into the 'hanging tree' for the flesh to set.

A few days later Terry sawed the carcase into quarters and hung it in the killing shed. I volunteered to cut the meat up for the dogs. It wasn't a big task as I was able to work on the quarters on the meat rail. The carcase was clean and very cold. I thought the meat looked far too good for the dogs. I cut out the fillet, the porterhouse and the rib eye. I took a piece of fillet to the house and seared it in a hot pan till it was just pink in the middle. It was tender, juicy, lean sweet meat, gourmet beef. What a waste to feed it all to the dogs. I wasn't sure where to find the rump steaks so I rang the butcher.

'You know the H-bone,' he said.

'You mean the pelvic bone where it joins the sacrum?'

'Um, well, do you have the rectum, know where that is?'

'Yes.'

'Well, take a line from where the porterhouse ended to the rectum and it's that bit of meat.'

'So it's the muscle from where the lumbar vertebrae end, and the sacrum begins, like where the last chop is?'

'Yeah, sort of.' The butcher was laughing. 'But you could call the medical centre if you like: they might be able to help.'

'No, I reckon I've got it. Thanks for all your help.'

'No worries,' said the butcher.

I think I found the rump steaks. After an hour's further dissection I had piles of prime stewing steak, wiener schnitzel and dog tucker which I bagged and chucked into the deepfreeze. The forequarters are hanging, ripening as we feed them to the dogs. Fresh meat is a rare treat for them. Their diet is predominantly dog biscuits, Mighty Mix and sheep meat, which has to be frozen on account of sheep measles/*taenia ovis*.

Dear Virginia

I couldn't be a farmer. We agreed that some time ago. I couldn't be a butcher either. But Bunsen eats meat and the garden is full of his cannon bones. I'm not consistent.

Already, the fast-growing seeds from the In trays have been transplanted into the garden. Virginia stocks, cornflowers, and turkestan salvia are sitting, startled-looking, in the newly exposed and cultivated soil. Far too many rocket plants make the transition and are growing lustily, loving the storms, wind and torrential rain. The tomatoes have been transplanted into individual pots — Fuel coffee paper cups are ideal for this. A quick fossick in the waste paper bins at work will provide enough coffee cups for all my spring plants.

The transplanted tomatoes, each in its own Fuel pot, are taken outside to be introduced to the big wide world when the weather's fine and still, and brought back inside to overnight in bug-free warmth. Back and forth they go, daily, as do basil seedlings. The idea is to harden them off without killing them from hypothermia or flattening them with gales. If I can commute to my work every day, they can commute to theirs.

When sowing very fine seed, like foxglove seed, scatter the seed in a pot, on top of moist soil. Tear a piece of newspaper the same size as the top of the pot, and soak it in water. Then place it on top of the seeds in the pot. Whenever the newspaper is dry, wet it a little, without moving the newspaper. Remove the paper when the seedlings are starting to push against it. This stops you knocking out the tiny seedlings with a rush of water. It keeps the seeds moist but not drenched, and keeps them warm.

I've planted Sun Cherry, Sun Gold and San Marzano. San Marzano is an Italian pear-shaped tomato, good for cooking because it's firm and not too juicy. The other two are cherry tomato hybrids, with bunches of tomatoes that hang in orderly trusses of 20 or so in a bunch, ideal for picking and eating, or for salads.

Some sweet williams, survivors from last year, and recently rediscovered under duvets of weeds, have Barbara Cartland pink flowers and now nestle on the soil like lap-dogs on cushions.

Claus, the man who laid the so-white concrete paths, has a wife who is an untwiner. She came to give him a hand on concrete pouring day. I rushed home at lunch time to check on progress. The concrete truck was blocking the lane at the bottom of the drive. Paths were being laid. Bunsen was locked inside so he couldn't walk on the concrete. Everything was in order except for one thing: the wife had untwined the yellow jasmine from the viburnum, up which it was growing. I watched out the window as she then started on the mandevilla. Twining plants seem to be able to twine once and once only. Once untwined, they don't start again. They just flop. I went out to ask her what she was doing. She said they would strangle the trees. It was at that very moment that Bunsen discovered the door was left open and came out to parade down the new, unset path. Claus, his untwining wife, and myself were all suddenly united in purpose. 'Get off!' we shouted at the badly confused dog who is trained to walk only on paths, never on the garden.

Dear Janice

Your landscaper woman, I picture as a sort of designer despot who stipulates with a Germanic rigour that thou shalt have lawn here, paths there — is she coming back to view the implementation of her design and will she be less than pleased at your unilateral decision to alter the plan? Good old Bunsen, imprinting the concrete with an indelible paw, just like the walk of fame in Hollywood.

I met a man called Hopeful Christian once. Well, I am Hopeful Gardener. I know it's too early but I have planted a row each of baby carrots, peas, baby beetroot and Cliff's Kidney potatoes. I also planted out a tray of mixed brassicas from the garden shop.

The front drive is awash with daffodils, 'fluttering and dancing in the breeze', all the way to the cattle stop. This weekend a Spring Festival is to be held in Hawarden, it used to be called The Plunket Flower Show and it has been held since forever. When the children were small and I was involved with Plunket I used to enter my daffodils in the show. This is how you show daffodils. You must cut multitudes of flowers the night before and then agonizingly and indecisively select the best blooms. All the reject daffodils fill every room in the house. Each bloom must be displayed in a glass bottle, I used sphagnum moss from the hills to stuff in the bottle neck to hold the blooms in place. In the morning I would put all the bottles in a milk crate, and gingerly slide the crate into the back of the car along with the baking for the cake stall.

Driving to shows and parties with a car full of flowers, baking or culinary arrangements which are not robust enough for winding gravel roads is part of country life. You drive very slowly round all the corners, in case of trucks, avoid pot-holes and gravel ridges and listen all the time for the sound of things crashing in the back seat or the boot.

Arriving at the flower show we competitors had to collect a competitor number and then go to the designated display area to place our blooms, you were then supposed to spend a long time twisting the bloom around in the bottle and massaging the petals and stems so that the flower would 'look at the judge'. I never took this part very seriously and I didn't ever make it out of the novice class. You were not allowed to compete in the novice class once you had won a number of points. I never won any. The competitors in the open class took the show very seriously; they would spend long moments on each bloom getting its face to look seductively at where the judge could catch its eye, they even stored flowers in the fridge prior to the show if they were opening too early. I didn't persevere with the daffodils; as the children grew I moved on to the PTA and Sausage Sizzles and Pet Days, and left daffodil showing to the next generation of Plunket mothers.

I was driving along Marshlands Road the other day. *Bleeding Hearts, $3.95*, the sign read and I wanted to stop and ask the man if they had been properly refrigerated but knew he would think I was mad. It would seem a lot easier to buy Bleeding Hearts for $3.95 a tray than to have a fridge stacked with trays of potting mix, but I suppose there is no challenge in just buying plants from a garden centre.

Dear Virginia

You're right. No challenge at all. Always make your job bigger than it needs to be: a lesson taught all Wellington civil servants at their mentors' knee, or workstation.

I like bulbs best in pots. Last September I had two bowls of daffodils on the front verandah, wide shallow bowls that I stuffed full of bulbs in the autumn. They looked great for a month. The bowls then rested over winter in the sleep-over bed down the side of the house, right in front of a four-wheel-drive. Then last week I noticed them because they were flowering! The same old soil in the same overcrowded pots — giving me their best show for two years in a row.

When planting bulbs I sprinkle sulphate of potash around — it promotes flowering.

The landscaper brought one gift to the garden — she showed me how to attach wire to the tops of posts and strain it taut with a nail twisted round and round. Works a charm. I've put high wires between all the posts, ready for the roses and vines and clematis to climb to. I've even put wires down the posts to help the plants climb. At the base of the new posts at the end of the garden I've planted: Louise Rowe, a white clematis, and Schuyler grape (black). They are at this moment twisting in torment in a gale. On the other post growing towards them is a black passionfruit, also, at the moment, looking tormented. On the posts at the end of the deck are François Juranville rose (nearly at the top of her post and onto the wire, if she can get through this storm). On the other end is Chasselas grape, green. It says on the name tag 'protect from wind'. Hmmm. It also says 'spray for mildew and black spot', so it might not be the plant for me. And a dark blue clematis. Albertine is now nearly at the new wire along the porch over the French doors. New Dawn, which for years has waved its long wands across the sky and occasionally along the washing line, is now restrained on a wire and growing along towards the passionfruit wire.

The roses have fared the worst in the rearranging of the garden. After I'd dug the roses up and put them in buckets, while the paths were being laid, I was reluctant to put them back. There seems no room for some of them now. Except for Graham T. I knew exactly where I wanted his new home to be. Of course I didn't label them all, on that crazy day when I pruned them back and stuck them in the buckets, so, inevitably, I don't know which is which. I've planted the one I think is Graham T, at the T intersection of the path, so I can look up from the kitchen sink and he's right there, at the end of the straight path. But what if the one I've planted is actually Mme Caroline Testout? Pink, instead of yellow, and not nearly so profuse. I will have to wait and see. But Sparrieshoop, and Raubritter? I just can't find places for them . . . The roses unaffected by the restructuring of the garden are Veilchenblau, Buff Beauty, Souvenir de la Malmaison, New Dawn, Complicata, August Gervais, Iceberg, Lady Hillingdon, Dublin Bay, Albertine, and François Juranville, Mme Caroline Testout, Nozomi, a couple of nameless ones friends have given me, Albéric Barbier, Mme Isaac Pereire, Gloire de Dijon — ah, just writing that list makes me realize I do probably have enough roses! They are all sprouting that soft, light-green foliage that is so lovely. I am aware this is the magic time, before the aphids arrive. When the torrential rain and gales finish I will put wires along the verandah in the front to guide Caroline, Gloire de Dijon, Albéric Barbier, New Dawn, and the wisteria. Oh, and the Albany Surprise grape on the garage.

Dear Janice

September ended with a raging snow-storm that transformed the farm into a snow field, Double Tops and Mt Lance looked like the southern alps. Another two inches of water fell into the rain gauge, there is mud everywhere, nature knows no moderation. We did enjoy the dry winter with no mud, but it seems there is a price to be paid for this little climatic convenience. The old proverb says the Lord giveth with one hand and taketh with the other. In secular parlance, there is no such thing as a free lunch.

You may have noticed, each month I write, that the weather has affronted me. Harry is much more phlegmatic. He adheres to the 'it is written' philosophy. If it is dry, he just says, 'We are one day closer to rain.' If it is wet he says, 'It'll dry up soon enough.' I keep old Omar Khayyam beside the bed to remind myself to be more accepting of the things I cannot change. I quote this verse.

> And that inverted Bowl we call The Sky
> whereunder crawling coop't we live and die,
> Lift not thy hands to It for help — for It
> Rolls impotently on as Thou or I.

I'm not really complaining about the rain, we needed it to fill the ponds and streams and swamps, but snow at the end of September is cruel and it is heartbreaking to see all the dead lambs, little flat white splodges lying on the green hills like empty cardigans. The snow fell wet and sticky, it clung to the bare trees, weighing down the branches, a big branch of the old silver birch snapped like a matchstick and crashed into the rhododendrons. The privet hedge looks as though the drunk hedge-cutter has returned — again — and the broad beans have fallen about all over the place. I rang Mandy to commiserate and we decided we were ready to leave for the city before the frost hits the roses.

Dear Virginia

We leave for London tomorrow so there will be a short break between garden letters. Robert has arrived. We have collected a perfect silver fern from Wilton's Bush to take to Boyd's grave.

It is lying flat at the bottom of my new suitcase. We'll return straight away. I'm not a traveller.

Dear Janice

You will have embarked on your pilgrimage by now. I will think of you visiting Boyd's grave. I wonder how that will be. Visiting graves is like listening for wind in the trees when you cannot be sure there is a wind. I always look for signs, I wish for a spiritual acknowledgement of my visit. At Cave Creek there is always a small grey Bush Robin hopping on his spindly legs at the top of the steps to the chasm. He is like a sentinel and that is enough.

Our loss was such a national event we had to watch TV to find out what was happening to ourselves, bizarre. I can't imagine how it must have been for you, to be left with private grief, a child, writing, and a career to manage.

October

Dear Virginia

I have returned. Robert has stayed for a while. West Ham cemetery is a beautiful, peaceful garden. It was good to be there and it is good to be back.

I was woken this morning by an insistent tapping, over and over, outside the window. I had to get up and investigate. I pulled the curtain open. Outside the window is the carport. Inside the carport, parallel to the house, is my car. A blackbird was dive-bombing the side mirror of my car, flapping, tumbling, refusing to land, then finally landing on the mirror's top, bending and pecking harshly at his own reflection. Over and over again. Then he flew off, spun round in mid-air before he reached the silver birch, and dived again, hitting the mirror in full flight. I let the curtain drop. The blackbird had showed me it was time to take charge of my life again. I threw bread, nuts and muesli out for the blackbird, and checked the roses for buds.

Dear Janice

Welcome back. I am sending you some 'hill kill' venison. The strawberries have set prolific sprays of fruit as they continue to flower. The apple is in full bloom, crawling with chimney bees on warm days. Three puppies are living in the apple tree enclosure, which used to be the hen run. Captain, Ebony and Meg are converting the steaks of the 'euthanized-in-childbirth cow' into puppy manure which will percolate through the soil to the roots of the apple tree. We will harvest and eat the apples, another link in the cycle of life and death that loops through all things.

October almost half over and the days more windy than still, the omens have been bad. One morning the men from Eco Pest rolled their truck off the road, and a shearer downed his handpiece after shearing three sheep and declared he would shear no more. Soon after lunch on that same day it began to sleet and in the midst of the storm Harry and I had to calve a heifer, delivering a shivering calf into a hail-drenched afternoon.

I made scones for the shearers this morning. I don't suppose baking a good scone has ever been a high priority in your life. Baking a good scone was not a priority of mine when we arrived at Double Tops. Scone making was a handicap to being a true feminist, so I never made scones, even for the shearers. My scones would have left a bad taste in the mouth anyway because they were always unskilful scones. There is a secret to scones, I've just discovered it and it does not come in a packet of ready-made scone mix but in a small carton of buttermilk.

Old Fashioned Scones

First stoke the woodstove till it is roaring, wait
two hours until the oven is very hot.

In the food processor, or a bowl, chop one ounce
of unsalted butter into three cups of high grade
pastry flour, add half a teaspoon of salt,
one teaspoon of sugar, one teaspoon of cream
of tartar and two teaspoons of baking soda.

Mix until the consistency of fine bread crumbs,
then add enough buttermilk to make a light dough;
don't overwork or the scones will be tough. Roll
out and cut square scones. Bake for as long as it
takes in a woodstove, which is about 15 minutes.

When I first made buttermilk scones Harry could not believe the scones were mine. When I first met him he said he was looking for a woman who could make a good scone. I thought I'd met a dinosaur. Now I'm the dinosauress. But, there you are. If you want to make good scones, forget the woodstove and the unsalted butter and the fine pastry flour. Just use buttermilk, a normal recipe and the electric oven. Spread the warm scones with whipped cream and jam.

Dear Virginia

I DO make scones, and because Boyd and I lived in America and I learnt to cook there, I've always used buttermilk. But my big secret is the perfect cream sponge. I know it is country women from North Canterbury who are the queens of cream sponges but I have an infallible recipe, given to me by my dear friend, William Taylor, who lives down a dirt track many k's out of Raurimu.

He makes cream sponges effortlessly while people talk, or while people walk on perfectly striped lawns, round his cypress- and rhodo-hedged garden. Here is the recipe.

Have all the ingredients measured before assembling, and have room-temperature eggs.
Sieve together these:

½ cup cornflour
2 tsp ordinary flour
1 tsp baking powder

Lightly grease 2 sponge pans and put cooking paper in the bottom.

Separate 3 eggs.

Beat whites till soft peaks.

Slowly add ½ cup caster sugar, beating all the time.

Add yolks and beat till a rich mixture.

Add all the sieved dry ingredients.

Divide into 2 pans and whack each pan firmly on the bottom.

Bake in pre-heated oven 180° for 15 minutes.

Whack each pan again when you remove them from oven.

Sit for 5–10 minutes before removing.

Fill sponge with fruit and whipped cream.

Eat immediately . . .

His lawn, by the way, is the largest, flattest, most stripey lawn I have even lain on. We have played croquet on it in the summer. Bunsen loves this lawn because it introduced him to the concept of the cocktail hour, and a life of lawn leisure which he is deprived of at home. While a group of us were lying around, drinking brandy alexanders out of wide cocktail glasses one hot summer evening, Bunsen strolled along licking the brandy out of every glass. We were too deep in an argument about croquet scoring to notice till he'd had about six.

While you are calving in sleet, and cooking perfect scones, I'm just spending this weekend watching the hyperactivity around me. Everything's exploding into growth. Oak tree leaves in the Botanic Gardens look as though they've crawled out of the ends of the branches, all crinkled up, thin as cigarette paper. There's a race on in my garden between Banksia and Souvenir de la Malmaison for first rose to bloom. There are small buds on all the roses.

Because growth is fast, my small and biodegradable cottage is in danger of being trapped in brambles like Sleeping Beauty's castle. Last October I hacked at yards of Albéric Barbier which grows a foot in every direction every day! Thank goodness I pulled that out. It would have covered the entire cottage by now. I still have Albéric growing over the front verandah, but as it's never watered, and the small bed's surrounded by concrete, I think its rampaging tendency will be thwarted.

Thank you for the venison. Someone at work was horrified I was eating meat that wasn't from the supermarket. He was seriously concerned I'd get some terrible disease, and he said I was breaking the law. I asked him if he'd ever lived in the country. He asked, 'Why would I?'

Dear Janice

Hyperactivity in your garden you say. Here it's the lawns. I turn my back on a lawn and within minutes it is a sea of yellow dandelions and daisies, the dandelion flowers turn to furry balls of fly-away seed and poof they are off in the wind to a new home. I mow the lawn every five or six days in the spring, a little and often is easier on the grass. I won't be relieved of the tyranny of the lawns and the noisy mower until midsummer.

Today we were shearing until two. After lunch I sped off down to the Weka Pass and finished a limestone carving course. When I got home and put my Henry Moore type 'form sculpture' on the lawn, Harry looked at it, tried to work out whether it was an elephant or a seal, and finally said, 'It will provoke a lot of discussion.' Mother used to sculpt but I did not inherit her artistic talents so I thought my shape rather an achievement with its smooth rounded lines, shadows and even a hole. (I don't think Penny Zino will ask me to exhibit at 'Art in a Garden' though. You have to come one spring to see all the sculptures in her garden. It is magnificent.)

Dear Virginia

I feel I was a bit oneupmanship-ish about the cream sponge. Sorry about that, but oneupmanship rules at the beginning of October. People stop me in the street on a dog walk and ask:

'Is your wisteria out? Your irises?'

'No.'

Then the point of the question is revealed, with: 'Oh, mine are.'

Next time I'm stopped I'll add to the mix: 'I'm thinking of getting a friend of mine to sculpt a piece for the back garden.' That'll shut them up.

Today I walked around my newly configured garden, feeling as though I didn't know it any more. I looked carefully at the familiar plants that hadn't been affected by the move. The stems of irises swell as thick as thumbs then suddenly this trivet-shaped flower appears, more giant insect than flower. Beautiful, blue and yellow. One iris is half out of its sheath, like a blue ice-cream in a cone. One of its strappy leaves is six feet long, trailing along the path. Aphids have arrived and are partying on Albertine.

After I'd done the look and learn exercise I felt better. I spread the new 'planting plan' on the ironing board and started transplanting my plants. First the camellia, pot-bound for all its life, is now where the rhubarb was, in front of Souvenir de la Malmaison (which has by far the biggest buds of all the roses — huge.) Next the bay was unpotted and planted next to what I think and hope is Graham T, right at the T intersection of paths. Then the rose that I hope is Raubritter went in, next to the clematis and grape on the new post. I also planted an old fishing rod, and tied Raubritter to that.

I put up wires along the side path, for the runner beans; two wires, top and bottom. The bottom one is a bit of a worry. You, I, a visitor, could trip over it. But it has to be there, to tie the vertical strings to. The weather was perfect. My tomatoes are starting to grow. They have been slow but 5 of them have their first green leaves now.

Dear Janice

It will be exciting to see your replanted roses as they bloom, interesting to see whether you have planted the right ones in the right places. I bought some roses last week, more than the pair of Icebergs I proposed buying earlier. I travelled to Cust where there is a rose nursery and have vowed to return in November when the roses are blooming, there are sweeping walks of rose garden and I imagine it will look and smell 'floriferously' magnificent then. You will be disgusted with me. I bought modern roses, the Icebergs which always thrive and two yellow florabundas, Eldorado and Royden. As you say, modern roses have boring names. I also bought a collection of red miniatures, I love red miniature roses growing amongst lavenders and catmint, the red and the blue look well together, I love the sultry look of strong colours, they suit the hot dry Virginia road sunshine, the watery wafting pinks and whites are out of character. So far we have evaded a serious frost so the roses are still covered in their first round of new leaves. No aphids yet.

Penny Zino, who is a rose grower of note, once told me it was very important to give the roses a dressing of dolomite lime some time over the winter. I forgot and hope that a spring application will suffice. I drove down to Pynes, the local farm-merchandising store in Hawarden and bought a 25 kg bag of dolomite lime. I put it on the farm account. That is another difference between city and country gardening. We have access to bulk supplies. I can buy so much of what I need in bulk. It makes environmental sense — no packaging — and it's much cheaper than garden centre prices. Lawn seed, fertilizers, weed killers; I buy them at Pynes and, the best bit, when I put it on the farm account it feels as if I haven't paid for it at all. We buy glyphosate (Round Up) in 200-litre containers for the farm. Glyphosate is sprayed onto the paddocks prior to grubbing or direct drilling, it saves ploughing and fallowing the soil. I have trouble coping with the concept that it is more environmentally friendly than ploughing, but the experts say that it is.

Anyway back to the roses and the dolomite which I applied for the first time ever. Someone told me a lime application is meant to make the bushes resilient to the worst ravages of blast. Is this a garden myth, I wonder? My roses always develop debilitating cases of blast after being frosted. I suppose I applied the lime too late, but I hope it may make some little difference. The roses also received two clean-up sprays with copper sulphate in the winter which, I hope, may also contribute to their good health. I will reserve judgement however until after the latest 'weather event' has cleared the country. Why aren't storms called storms any more? It was trying to snow this morning and two days of fine frosty weather are predicted to follow on. Frosts at this time of the year sorely test me.

Dear Virginia

I bushwhack along the path at the back of the garden, between the graffiti of blossoming yellow Banksia all over the new fence, and the marching army of catmint on the other side, with its cohorts all gleaming in purple and gold. I see a cricket ball nestled in the top of the artichoke I'd cunningly planted last year right in the middle of the path, between paving stones. It's a wide plant but only knee-high at present so it is possible to climb over it. As I do just this, I bend to pick up the ball, to throw it back to the neighbours. It isn't a cricket ball. It is magenta-coloured, round, and hard-looking, but it is an artichoke, a new addition to the garden, as dramatic an entry as the crowning of a baby's head at birth. I stand there, amazed.

Did you know artichokes are thirsty plants? Water them a lot. They love seaweed soup. The globe artichoke is one of the oldest cultivated vegetables.

Robert, overzealously clearing the gutters, has cut the wisteria off at ground level. 'Getting into the gutter,' he explained. 'A weed.'

Dear Janice

I have the strangest recipe for artichokes. I found it in an old book, *The Alice B Toklas Cook Book*. The recipe is called 'Hearts of artichokes à la Isman Bavaldy'. It involves cooking 12 artichokes with lemon and cardamom then extracting the hearts, making a purée of sweetbreads and boiling three pounds of asparagus. The assembly of the dish involves standing the asparagus up in the centre of the artichoke heart and packing the puréed sweetbread around it, and after that covering everything with bread crumbs and baking a further 15 mins in the oven. At the end of the recipe Alice B says that this dish does not take as long to prepare as it sounds and she says that the coriander and lemon give it 'an ineffable flavour'.

This morning three swallows were looping over the swimming pool, and what do they say about two swallows not making a summer? Well, in my book if there are more than two it is a sign that summer is on the way.

Write to me of billowing roses, tomatoes climbing up bamboo stakes, lettuces basking in the summer sun. Even if it is not true, I want to believe that it is summer somewhere.

Dear Virginia

Summer? Well, what about roses growing so fast they seem more animal than plant? There's François on Pole 1, with a wire stretching taut from Pole 1 to Pole 2, to its north. There's Albertine on Pole 3, with a wire stretching taut to Pole 2, to its west. Right? These two roses are both growing towards Pole 2. Having finished my book about Antarctic whaling I can now relax and watch my own version of a race to the pole. Which rose will win? Which will starve and die? François has started off more strongly but the northerly blows her back. Albertine is slower but she's creeping constantly forward. I swear she grows in the night.

I'm desperate for soil space for the seedlings in the In trays. I tug giant borage trees out of the soil. Catmint spreads like ripples on a pond. Every day it has swallowed up more blue cranesbills, campanulas, bergamot, cornflowers, pansies, poppies. It is in October that I wish, I wish, I had a larger garden. On this one sunny weekend in October I imagine planting a gravel drive with flowering cherries. Under them catmint, tides of it, spreading, spreading. Islands of lavender. At the back, upright Tuscan Blue rosemary. At the very edge of the gravel, California poppies, maybe a ribbon of daffodils between the poppies and the blue sea of catmint. But it's only a dream. Instead of admiring a sweeping drive and arching trees, I hurl campion clumps onto the skyscraper compost pile. I add fennel, forget-me-nots, California poppies, sweet peas, chervil. I cut back the rosemary.

I carry out search and destroy missions. The dreaded convolvulus is back, winding its way around everything. Wandering Willie colonizes under other plants' leaves. I don't mind him much. He's easy to pull out. Insidious convolvulus is different. Its snake-like white roots travel right across a garden bed back to its homeland in the neighbour's. I don't use chemicals. I just personally meet and greet every weed and pull them out. Convolvulus I consign to a Pak 'n' Save shopping bag, from where it goes to the rubbish bin. I don't compost it.

Snails and aphids and greenfly are illegal immigrants. I do a dawn raid to wipe rose buds clean of bubbly insect froth. Snails chew the passionfruit leaves. Every night I go out to do my feeling frenzy; in the dark I feel the leaves, each one, removing snails as I go.

Dear Janice

I have never seen a snail at Double Tops, I think it must be too cold. Why don't you cook and eat your snails instead of squashing them? I'm sure I could find you a recipe from *Alice B Toklas*. I'm glad I do not have to stand guard against creeping convolvulus. I would not meet convolvulus with a pitch-fork or whatever feeble instrument of destruction you have at your disposal. I would be out in the dead of night heavily disguised as a terrorist and I would poison it with a weapon of mass destruction. Amitrole would be my weapon of choice.

I like October rain, if it's gentle. It highlights the soft tree-green of spring and enhances the smell of plants growing. The leaves of the birches and willows are the palest lime green, the new poplar leaves smell sweet and sticky and the weeping elm is festooned with blooms which are like clusters of pale green tissue paper. Under the trees on the walk to my dog kennels the hostas are poking through the leaf mould like unfurled umbrellas. They will gradually unroll themselves into clusters of blue-green leaves. The most forward of the rhododendrons is flowering. The pale pink trumpet-like flowers are so pretty, but it is a foolhardy plant for such exhibitionism will be punished. Every spring, frosts turn the pretty pink flowers to slush.

In the vegetable garden the baby carrots and beetroot are just visible, potato leaf tips are breaking the soil, the white and black broad bean flowers are opening. The strawberries are festooned with white and yellow flowers, I will cover them on frosty nights, as frosts kill the flowers and stunt the new berries. October is the time of year when there is nothing to eat in the garden except silverbeet and that has to be covered in bird netting because the sparrows fancy it too.

Dear Virginia

No snails! I dream of such a place!

I've planted out my molly-coddled tomato seedlings. They're sturdy things, with four large leaves on each. Upright, green, hairy — like macho aliens. I don't want them to get stem wilt, be eaten, be sat on by the cat, be blown over by the equinoctial gales. So each beautiful plant has an Agee preserving jar, or a large pickle jar, or, God forbid, a plastic storage container, upturned over it. Personalized greenhouses for the young. Beside each ungainly shelter is a bare bamboo pole, 6 feet high. The garden looks unlovely, workaday but optimistic.

The mail shed garden at the bottom of the drive turns into a triumph of muddled blue and waving yellow. It's knee-deep in flowers. Shiny yellow flowers of frothy California poppies, with chunky blue borage, felicia, blue daisies, yellow daisies, and the orange Iceland poppies. The poppies look great here. They aren't competing with a mound of pink daises or yellow roses as they are in the garden proper. Viscaria and carnations sway in amongst it all. And there, almost hidden by a shoulder of catmint, is a most beautiful white flower, the first Alfred Carrière! It's large, white, floppy, very perfumed. I am so happy about it. I pick it for the coffee table. I hope there are many more. I give the plant a watering-can of water, a rare treat for mail shed dwellers.

Jasmine is showing through again too. It's a comeback queen. The cabbage tree looks down at the swirl of it all, even though the poor tree has been knocked sideways by 'the squeezer' again.

The path of flagstones I laid to lead the postie to the slot on the mail shed door is buried under flowers. He has to either high-step over the clumps, or just bulldoze his way through. I'm never there when he arrives so I don't know how he solves the problem, but he doesn't tread on the flowers, and I do still get mail. I can imagine it's not a pleasant journey when the plants are clingy with rain.

October is the month of chaos. At the moment wind-blown hail is battering the small tomato seedlings. The trees look as though they are being thrown around the garden. The whole garden looks staunch, but miserable. I anchor pot plants down by putting large cast-iron saucepans on top of the soil to stop them blowing over again. Complicata, a pink, simple rose — yes, I didn't name her . . . has folded its four flat petals over, like a damp envelope. The irises are horizontal. The orange poppy petals are all ripped off by the gales, but the early roses enjoy being tossed around. Souvenir de la Malmaison likes its absurdly full blooms whipped about by hair-dryer winds. If the air's still, those blooms turn to mush on a stem, a disgusting sight, like brown sodden paper tissues.

One good thing about October weather is that it produces lots of blooms for vases. I rush outside after work, in that hour that daylight-saving has brought, and rescue new iris blooms, roses, stocks, from the raging storm and bring them in to safety. I don't take any to work. Crossing the motorway bridge is almost impossible in a storm. I need to cling to the railing. With a briefcase in one hand and a bunch of flowers in the other, teetering on high-heeled shoes, streamlined in a straight skirt, I'd probably take off and end up smeared across someone's windscreen many feet below.

Mme Caroline Testout is open on the verandah. She is so very beautiful. Barbara Cartland pink (oh no!) but such a perfect shape she can carry the colour, which is more than you could say about Barbara Cartland . . . Several stems rise high, up to the roof. One bends over to the garage, and will be an archway between garage and veranda by the end of the summer. Two stems are bent along the whole length of the verandah railing. Each of these horizontal stems has scores of fat buds and already some huge railway-cup-shaped flowers.

My 'to do' list grows taller than the struggling tomato seedlings:

- make up hosta pots for the front verandah
- make two new composts with horse manure gathered from Alison and David's farm
- put up bean strings
- plant sunflowers
- transplant all the rest of the tomatoes
- cosset the basil seedlings.

But, hey, it's pouring with rain, cold, windy again. No more gardening will be done in October. Time to read another gardening book.

Dear Janice

I know I've said this before but when I go out to work I do not have to wear silly clothes that are unsuited to cold, windy, rainy spring days as you do, which means that if I want to pop into the garden for half an hour's weeding I don't need to change my clothes. Work and gardening are interchangeable, not like you. Down on the farm we are much more practical and less attuned to looking elegant; I wear jeans, boots, a jersey, hat and always my dog whistle. I wear a tinted sunscreen moisturizer — for my crinkled skin — lipstick and earrings. It just reminds me that I'm a woman in a bloke's world.

You must always have to change from your work clothes to gardening clothes, unless you are playing Lady Marriott of the Manor, languidly wandering the paths plucking blooms to put in your trug and being careful not to let the thorny rose bushes ravage your nylons. Talking of being ravaged, whatever happened to the squeezer and the cat-flap molester?

November

Dear Janice

Yesterday morning Harry shook me awake at two, hissing 'The sky is clear.' A southerly storm had been blowing at full fury when we went to bed. I hate southerly storms that drag no lingering tail of cloud. I stumbled out of bed, wrapped my prickly Swanndri around my bare body, and slipped gumboots onto my cold-brittle feet. Outside the sky was an inverted bowl of black, glittering with diamonds and cold. The wind had died. The garden table sparkled with furry ice crystals. Together, my gallant Harry and I covered the precious flowering strawberries and the potatoes with sheets of heavy plastic. I apologized to the roses as the sap stopped flowing in their veins, and went back to bed.

In the morning the soft new rose growth drooped and a couple of days later the tell-tale black wilt began to creep down the soft stems to the hard wood. Rose gardeners all round the district are exchanging blast horror stories. Like little old ladies comparing the severity of our varicosities, we discuss the extent to which our roses have been infected by blast. Struck down with a blast episode you must seize the secateurs and surgically remove the diseased foliage. The foliage must be burnt. You must sterilize the secateurs. Another rose aficionado says it is prudent to spray with cupric oxychloride. You can do this before a blast episode and it will afford some protection, he says. Why is it called blast? I can think of much better words like #@**& and #@*&*.

Dear Virginia

No frost here, just wind and rain. Wind that rocks everything — new pear tree, little mizuna seedlings, mulch, the very house. We have had nothing but wind for three weeks. The only thing that thrives in it is weed seeds, flung into all corners of the garden, probably airborne, express delivery, from Auckland.

Today, a work day, it was very hot at lunch time. The spindly stems of the tomato seedlings drooped inside their individual bottle greenhouses so I removed the bottles. I watered the seedlings, then rushed back to work. When I returned home at 6, the sky had blackened, the temperature dropped. I checked the tomatoes. I started tucking one plant's leaves under the rim of its Agee preserving jar for the night. Then I thought better of it. Nah, I told it. You don't want those leaves confined in a bottle overnight, do you? The tomato nodded at me. I went back inside to make dinner. Within minutes, it started hailing. I stood in the kitchen, watching hailstones bounce, splinter and cover the deck. The foxgloves were battered down. The roses' petals dropped. The Dublin Bay arch, already top-heavy with blossoms, bent lower and lower so that now only a cat could regard it as an archway. And the tomato seedlings? Well, I haven't been out to check. I don't want to know. I'm writing to you instead.

Dear Janice

You are a neglectful mother, poor little tomatoes. In the garden our November is most likely akin to your October; your hyperactivity in October, that is us in November. The farm and garden compete for my time. The farm always takes priority. As a shepherd I cannot say to Harry, 'Sorry but I can't come tailing today. The garden needs me.' Poor garden. I can barely keep pace with the enthusiasm of the plants. The lawn keeps growing and growing. It needs mowing every five days to look civil. I don't mind too much if I have to leave it a week; it looks unkempt before it is mown, but the daisies look pretty and there are yellow buttercups in the wet spots! Do you remember the buttercup test? When we were at school together we would test to see whether people liked butter by holding a buttercup under their chins. If the flower threw a golden glow under the chin they were cast as butter lovers.

November is tailing month. My spirits sink at the start of every tailing season as I contemplate clipping the ears of three-thousand-plus lambs. Since my second back operation I only muster and ear-mark. Tailing is not as physically demanding as it used to be but the boredom is difficult to manage. I must never let my thoughts wander from lambs' ears. Left clip for a ewe lamb, right for a ram lamb. It's very hard to maintain concentration on such an intellectually absorbing task!!

Last Friday was one of those days when I should have gone back to bed and started over — the Feng Shui was all wrong. A nor'wester rattled the morning. At six Harry instructed me to 'make a morning tea and be at the Peninsula yards by nine, and you won't need dogs'. At seven thirty, three painters arrived to paint the roof. John arrived to prune the shrubberies at eight. The phone kept ringing. There were no biscuits for the morning tea. The yearling calves broke into my tree lane and Very Annie Mary, my calf, kicked me. I flung myself into the red Niva at ten to nine and roared away up the lane to find Harry and Sam bleeding air out of the water system in the O'Riordan trough. After all my rushing and panic, they were not even ready to

begin tailing! I should have driven home, let my dogs off and rounded up the sheep, but I didn't. I drove down to the pond and thought, bugger, I'm just going to lie here and look at the sky until they *are* ready. And I did.

The birds fled when I arrived, alerted by the 'stranger, danger' screech of the paradise ducks. After lying still for five minutes or so I watched the ducks waddle back to the water's edge with their ducklings. The pukekos strutted out of the reeds with their chickens, little balls of bright-blue fluff on spindly stilts, the black teal glided from their refuge in the south arm of the pond to float silently on the brown water and a hare loped across the earth dam. He stood still for a minute, twitched his nose and loped on into the matagouri on the far side of the pond.

My mind slowed as I contemplated life as a duck: to have no concept of yesterday and no expectation of tomorrow, to hatch from an egg and live the rest of your life negotiating death. The wind still whistled through the fence wires and sang in the grass heads but I didn't feel turned inside out any more. I thought, how dreadful to live forever in the city, to never escape from the bustle of human activity. How do you find peace if you cannot take yourself off and let a spring morning wash over you for a while?

Dear Virginia

I think of peace as stepping off the treadmill, not having to do anything for anyone, not having to be conscious of the passing of time, being absorbed. I find peace in a city on a dog walk. This is not like a muster. I don't expect Bunsen to round up stray cats. We just wander. I find peace watching Bunsen roll over and over in the Botanic Gardens, his grin seeming to slide off his face into the grass. What do people do, who don't have dogs to give them an excuse to hurl sticks into the surf? But also, I garden when I want peace. Each weekend I set out into the tiny plot, regardless of storms. In November I crouch close to the soil, like a child, and enjoy fiddling with tiny seedlings, seeds, soil. I don't notice the continual hum of traffic on the motorway, so it's peaceful enough. If some neighbour's music is blasting out, or mower is roaring, I just have to ignore that. I'm bent on providing food, flowers, and foliage. Providing plenty. Maybe women are hard-wired to do this?

I water small plants, divisions, cuttings, bits from other people's gardens, seedlings, transplants. All are delicate, all ringed with hope. Gardeners are good project managers. They don't miss deadlines. The seasons don't wait for you.

I sow into trays (the In trays from the office) because seeds get lost or eaten, or trodden into oblivion by huge Labrador paws, if they are planted straight out into the garden. I have tomatoes, basil and zucchinis in pots at the moment. Today, 11 Nov, I started transplanting them. This is very like sending your small child off to school for the first time. You wave goodbye. They are out in the big wide world now. You can only wait and hope they get through the day, and the subsequent days, safely. I hate turning my back on those little plants and going back indoors — particularly if a storm's blowing through.

November is when the whole garden gets tangled up in

convolvulus — if I let it. It comes in under the fences. The whippy stem knits up every ravelled sleeve of every plant in the whole garden. I rip it out, knowing that one big blitz on it in November will 'train' it for the year.

Other colonizers are borage and forget-me-not but I like removing them. Borage is so big, and coarse. One satisfying tug and the whole plant comes out, clean. Forget-me-not is now past its best. It forms a mat which is easily pulled out. One small root and the plant mat can be 1 metre square. When I go back inside I'm covered in bidibids — forget-me-not seeds. I think it's called forget-me-not because it's hard to forget that little plant when you are covered in tiny round burrs. Nasturtiums run rampant too, but I let them clamber around under the apple tree. They are supposed to deter codlin moth.

Dear Janice

We wage war against weeds in the spring too. Spring-time is when the gorse and broom plants reveal themselves out on the hills. They dress up in bright yellow flowers and stand out amongst the crowd. When we muster for tailing we carry little backpacks containing plastic containers full of Tordon prills to sprinkle on any plants we find. I love killing gorse and broom. How I curse the English settlers who brought it with them to remind them of home. I am very careful with the prills, I respect Tordon. Harry cannot understand why I yell if he muddles the Tordon pack with the lunch pack. The lunch pack is orange and must not be used for Tordon. Apart from its toxicity I'm sure it wouldn't taste nice.

Dear Virginia

What are prills???

Last night I was snuggled up in bed reading an old *National Geographic* about the circulating presents of New Guinea islanders. Like a hobbit's precious mathoms, they are treasured gifts that are passed around the community. Plants are my version of them. This weekend I visited the sister of a friend, who has a garden of sun and sand at Lyall Bay, on the coast. She showed me a fig that she'd got from her sister, who'd received it from me because my garden isn't big enough for a fig. I'd been given it by David at Pauatahanui. He'd grown it from seed. She had an avocado that was a cutting from one I'd given her sister too — another tree that would be too big for me.

Dear Janice

Prills are pills with an R, the R makes them run. Seriously, Tordon prills are fine granules of poison. They look like fawn semolina and they smell nasty. They are ideal for poisoning rogue gorse or broom bushes out on the hills. It is mid November, Canterbury's show week. The show weekend is a bench-mark; as Anzac Day is to broad beans, so show weekend is to tomatoes. Conditions are said to be dangerous for tomatoes before the weekend and safe after it. But not this year: the mountains are winter mountains, the winds are cold.

Weather Workshop warns of frosts, or maybe an ice event? The tomatoes I sowed in seed boxes in September are only three inches high so I have purchased two well-grown tomato plants from a nursery in town. I will grow them in pots on the terrace. Both plants are flowering. Is this cheating?

Do you remember the cauliflower, broccoli and cabbage mixture which I planted in September? Well, they have gone. My beloved Harry left the little orchard gate open. The pet sheep walked through it out onto the back drive, in through the garden gate and pigged out on the vegetable garden. Luckily for Harry, he spotted the pets from the kitchen window before they had reached the peas, otherwise I may have shot him. Harry was quite the model of insouciance; I extracted an apology which he did not feel. Harry is a pragmatist. 'Vegetables, like bad hair cuts, regrow,' he said. The sheep did not take even an exploratory bite of the broad beans. This says something very significant about broad beans, I think. It says that they are not very nice to eat, that one must acquire a taste for them when one has grown up and knows that they are, currently, a fashionable vegetable written about in magazines like *Cuisine*.

The mesclun mix is growing taller — the sheep were not partial to that either. It will soon be ready to stand a light haircut with the scissors. The first sowing of potatoes is pressing valiantly on, after being singed by the frost. The spring sowing of Florence fennel is due to be transplanted into the garden; I will sow another tray of seed for later in the summer. The sweet corn seeds have sprouted under an old window frame; I'm trying two new varieties from the Kings Seed catalogue, Hopi Blue a traditional Indian blue corn, and Honey and Pearl. I will plant a second sowing this week. The secret of summer vegetable gardening is to have a succession of vegetables maturing all season. To achieve this you need to plant small amounts of seeds regularly throughout spring and early summer. Some gardeners have the idea that you sow the summer vegetable garden in the spring, all at once; but if you do that all the vegetables ripen at the same time and you are faced with a feast you cannot eat. My way is time-consuming, but if you love watching seeds grow into a succession of beautiful vegetables it is a source of endless pleasure.

The later-flowering rhododendron buds are bound tight, pointed like candle flames perched amidst a floret of leaves, soon they will be bursting open into a blaze of hot pink and white, a glorious celebration of late spring. I do not know my rhododendrons by name, though they are not a large family. Two were here when we came and the rest I have introduced as room has become available. After John hacked into the old shrubbery I found room for three new ones. I always choose the plants that flower late in the season, to cheat the frost. I have one funny little rhododendron named Parisienne. She has pretty little round furry leaves and when she flowers the blooms are waxy pale lemon trumpets. Parisienne is the spring barometer. She begins the winter with a full compliment of buds. They are greenish and yellow, and as the winter grows into spring they should begin to swell and turn a pale lime yellow. If the season is kind, half the buds turn pale lime yellow and half of them freeze at the base, turn brown and fall. If the season is very unkind, they all drop off. This spring Parisienne will not be flowering. One year, and I forget just which year, Parisienne was yellow all over like a pale lemon fountain. That is why I keep her on.

The bush roses are still weeks from flowering. The climbers

are more inclined to risk blooming. Their elevation protects them from frost burn. The dwarf irises have almost finished. If you forget to wander in the garden you might miss a dwarf iris, they are transient flowers. The bearded iris buds are beginning to unroll. I love irises. You need to peer into the depths of an iris to appreciate their voluptuous colours, the regal plush, the velvety purples and maroons, the little furry tongues on the fall of the petals. They are sensuous flowers.

Dear Virginia

Your roses are so valiant fighting against frost. Mine are just making me impatient. When is my Veilchenblau going to develop buds? There's no sign yet at all. All the other roses are either flaunting themselves, or at least in bud. The best, by far, is Mme Isaac Pereire — very smelly indeed, dark purple, exactly the same colour as the valerian it grows with. It has a beautiful shape, and it opens fully. After a few days the centre pushes forward and the rose looks as though the wind's blowing it all back. Strange, but this enables it to scent the air even more. I wish it was in a more prominent place than beside the garage! I've delighted in the very smelly Albertine, with its bright pink buds, the carnation-looking François Jeranville (not as great as I thought), and August Gervais (white, floppy, and apricotty). I'm still waiting for Mme Alfred Carrière to put her head up above the nepeta. Surely any self-respecting rambler should be able to grow higher than nepeta!

Dear Janice

As I write, it is a cold, damp afternoon. A starling has been flying back and forth with its beak full of worms for its young in a nest under the roof. It keeps a wary eye on me as it sits on the guttering. If I remain still it crawls in to the nest. If I move it flies into the birch tree and waits until I stop tapping. I can hear a shining cuckoo whistling. They come to lay their eggs in the grey warbler nests in the late spring. The cuckoo chick pushes the warbler chicks out of the nest and poor old Mr and Mrs Warbler feed it until it is big enough to fly away. The bellbirds are sipping grevillea nectar which they share with swarms of bees on bee-flying days. I don't know about bellbird nests. I find nests belonging to blackbirds and thrushes in the bushes when I'm pruning, and hedge sparrows' nests in the hellebore plants which always seems an absurdly low place to hatch out a family safely. Swallows nest in the old cow bale beside Kit's pond, and starlings nest in nooks and crannies around all the buildings. They are the messiest nest-builders you ever saw. They strew unkempt piles of plant litter on shelves. They have no idea of weaving a round, neat nest at all.

The strangest 'nest' is a plover's nest, a sprinkle of litter on the ground in the middle of a paddock with three green and brown speckled eggs. This year a pair of plovers built a nest in the middle of the sheep yards. During the hogget shearing I insisted that we work around the plovers' nest and so it survived until a week later when a fat Oxford ram jumped into the yard to eat the luxuriant grass. He smashed the eggs. I found the half-grown embryos strewn and the parents gone. Life is hard in the bird world.

I was watching a blackbird's nest built in a bag hanging in the garden shed; the eggs hatched, the little chicks began growing feathers, then one morning I found blackbird feathers on the floor, evidence of a struggle. In the nest only one mutilated chick remained, a stoat is the most likely culprit. The stoat traps have been baited with eggs.

Dear Virginia

Today my spring garden looks so young, shiny, disease-free, optimistic. And there are so many flowers out. Geums, clematis, all the roses, larkspur, campanulas, cranesbills, rhodos, camellias just finishing, white ladies, pinks, lychnis, California poppies, lavender, verbascum, stocks (which flower for longer than any other flower I know), foxgloves (6 feet high, although now angled about 30 degrees from the ground because of the wind), bishop's flowers, cornflowers, daisies — yellow ones, white ones — corydalis, pansies, and the first shasta daisies.

I'm still unsatisfied. I dream of a border of tall bishop's flowers and nicotianas (sylvestre) with poppies and artichokes.

I have planted a new tree tomato. I staked it with a macrocarpa rail and a bamboo. It's windy out there. I hope it survives. Behind it I've sown sweet peas (old ones, Kings Seed) and plan to plant sunflowers in front of them. Penstemons are in the long foxglove bed. Clary sage is in front of the new clematis and grape post.

Spinach is looking good, crinkly, shiny, clean and green. Three tomatoes are holding their own in the cold, windy garden.

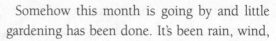

Somehow this month is going by and little gardening has been done. It's been rain, wind, occasionally very hot, but never settled. I have tied the tomatoes to their bamboo stakes. I've watched the beans trying to wrap themselves round the strings, fighting the wind, which untwines them. I've watched one Black Beauty zucchini survive that first week transplanted into the garden in a storm that blew it round and round, so fast the speed put the snails off regarding it as a revolving restaurant.

I have adored the huge, teapot-sized artichokes. I couldn't eat them! The globes are opening now slightly, like a bowl, and there will be a purple bristle flower inside. I have planted out some basil. I've sadly pulled out all the old spinach that got me through the winter. It just kept resprouting, more and more leaves all the time. There is too much rocket — all gone to seed (I love the flowers). Lots of chives, parsley, mint.

But in truth I haven't had enough time to wallow in the garden this month. Weekends have been taken up with socializing, working, or sheltering inside out of the teeming grey rain. The new concrete is covered with sodden rose petals and looks as old as a ruin.

Dear Janice

Show week has been and gone. It is a gloomy Sunday, a winter's day. Deep and dark November skies are lowering over the hills, shedding snow and ice balls on the garden. The mountains when I caught a glimpse amidst the shifting clouds are white to below the timber line. But the talk of drought has been suspended. The brown ridge lines have greened down on the lower country, where the farmers' eyes were beginning to crinkle with worry as they looked to the horizon for rain.

Dear Virginia

In November I should be around for the garden. I should do lots of maintenance tasks every day. Check the snails aren't eating the zucchini seedlings. Check the tomatoes aren't too dry. Check the newly transplanted sunflowers. Are they drooping? Water them. Water everything. The long hose follows me around the garden like a pet snake. It often cuts corners, or sidewinds the width of paths. Either way it crushes small plants. Weeds appear overnight, especially chickweed. Weed the seedlings. Weed the sweet peas. Train the roses and passionfruit along the wires that they seem to be avoiding. Have the beans come up yet? The sweet peas? After a couple of weeks of this pressure, the 'to do' list is too long to be achievable. It's time to take a day off work, and get into the garden. Call it a Spring Day on my Annual Leave Form.

Bees are burrowing in the foxgloves. They prefer the speckled pink ones to the white ones, I notice. Maybe this is why the pink ones are more common on the hill.

Dear Janice

The rhododendrons are in full bloom, one a cascade of pink like a waterfall under the birch tree. A huge crimson peony is flowering and it has engulfed the primroses which will have to be rescued. All over the garden the aquilegias are blooming. At the back door old-fashioned pink, yellow and white flowers are swaying on long thin stems. They have been growing there for fifty years. In the borders around the front of the garden the aquilegias are smaller, dark blue, purple, pale pink, dark pink. They match and mate producing blue, pink and purple variations of infinite variety. I like to call them columbines. The name has a softer ring, a magic sound to go with harlequin. You must cut the spent flower-heads off your columbines else you will have them sprouting like weeds in every bare space in the garden. The catmint stems are beginning to bud the faintest blue. They will open to bright blue in the next few weeks. Dutch irises have unfolded. They are longer-lasting than the bearded variety. You can cut them for flower arrangements if you are a cut-flower person. I have tried to grow a range of colours but the yellow and whites have not survived. The dark blue strain is the hardiest. They add slashes of electric colour to the rose bed. Along the kitchen garden fence another variation on blue, the first delphiniums are flowering at a funny angle. The budding spikes rose into the wind and were blown over; the sun lured them up again into a right-angled turn towards the light. The flowers are inky purple blue. Next year I promise they will be staked.

December

Dear Virginia

My rhodo has thrips, which results in a silvering of the leaves, but there's an up-side to everything. At night it looks like Katherine Mansfield's silver pear in 'Bliss'. Appropriate as she was born just down the road.

'Green fingers are the extension of a verdant heart,' said Russell Page. Very nice, but what of squashed thumbs? I dropped a railway sleeper on my green thumb today, so there will be no more writing for a while.

Dear Janice

Thank you for writing to say that you cannot write because you have squashed your thumb under a railway sleeper. I'm terribly sorry about your thumb. It must hurt, but I'm so pleased that you have written because now I have an excuse to write back in reply.

If you owned a tractor you would not have squashed your thumb. I shudder to think of a time when a big tractor will not be at my disposal. Many parts of the garden are not accessible by tractor, deliberately on my part, as the thought of tractors and bulldozers ravaging the garden was disturbing when I first began gardening. However, as I have grown older I have conceded the tractor has its uses. The tractor saves the ageing body from ruin. Last weekend I asked Harry to remove a branch from a Thuya Rheingold which has grown for twenty-five years against the front wall of the garage. A grapevine had become enmeshed between the crevices of the Thuya's drooping feathery branches and a nasty little strangulating native creeper had also insinuated itself amongst the confusion of foliage. Harry only consents to assist in the garden if a tractor or a chainsaw is able to be employed. After one branch had been removed we had to remove another to balance the bush. This did not improve the aesthetics of the bush either. The bush had to go. Harry went off for the tractor. He returned with the beast and a big heavy metal chain. Harry manipulated the chain and I drove the tractor, and together we removed the poor old Thuya in two minutes. Now there is a big ugly bare hole in front of the garage. The garage will have to be painted and the garden rearranged.

Dear Virginia

I can see how tractors help you. Maybe I'll add one to my Christmas wish list, just a very small one. A mini tractor would have been handy when I tried to remove a clump of agapanthus. I love the flowers, and the glossy, strappy leaves, but try getting rid of them and they turn out to be the worst sort of garden tenants. I dug and tugged all morning and was astounded by the amount of root mass. I severely strained myself. But I got over it. Much worse, if we're talking about damage to the body, is the damage caused by dancing too much at the staff Christmas party in the Botanic Gardens last Friday night. While Bunsen justified the hiring of expensive caterers and ate everything within his reach, I danced to the great music of our staff band (a truly exceptional band of musos and singers) and could not get out of bed the next day! One hip was so sore I couldn't put any weight on it for two days. I am still hobbling.

This is very embarrassing. Added to the bandaged thumb, I look war-wounded.

Yesterday was one hot day, after days of rain and wind. And this magic day bloomed on a weekend. It was a day of pause, of stillness. The deck was too hot to walk on with bare feet. It was too hot to garden. I just went around, introducing myself to plants I hadn't seen for a while. How do you do? My, you've grown. That sort of thing. No staking, weeding, trimming, picking. Just being there, part of it. I watered the pathetic-looking zucchini — Black Beauty. Have faith, I said to it. You will enjoy it here.

I discovered my sunhat is too big. It falls over my eyes. Has my head shrunk since last summer? Or did the straw hats expand over the winter hanging on the newel post at the bottom of the stairs? I also discovered you can't be on the cordless phone *and* wearing a sunhat. There's no room for the phone's aerial under the hat.

But, as the sun sloped away towards the hill, the need to control and change got the better of me and my meditations. One-handedly, I yanked out 5-feet-high flowering silverbeet. I couldn't pull out the ancient onions because they are now slipping off their paper-thin cowls, shaped like turbans, and flowering with giant heads of mauve explosions. A small ginger cat, looking up at such a flower, would see a huge firework in the sky.

I said to a visiting friend, as we walked up the drive, 'Isn't it wonderful, what the garden will look like next year?' It was a gardeners' comment. She knew what I meant.

I am still waiting for my Veilchenblau to bloom like a daisy bush. I'm losing faith that it will ever be covered in many purplish flowers. Alfred Carrière on the mail shed is drowned in the mauve sea of nepeta. I cut a breathing hole for it. A friend has bought a Graham Thomas. She keeps referring to him as Thomas Graham. I told her to think of g and t's and that way she'll get the order right.

December is the month for gardeners' OOS or RSI or whatever they now call it. I dead-head and trim and lightly prune. My (other) thumb and first finger joint feel as stiff as unoiled secauteurs. I cut till I can't cut any more. I think of you tagging lambs' ears — real lambs, not the plants with the grey furry leaves. Complicata is a mass of brown spiders — that's what the ends of the flowers now look like. Raubritter is worse. Her tight pink flowers become brittle, brown curls, like wood shavings. They just sit there, and I have to remove them, every one.

Dear Janice

I have to tell you about *my* Veilchenblau. Poor lady, she lost her grip on the picket fence during a heavy rainstorm and drooped to the ground over the garden path to the back door. Harry growled and grizzled. He threatened to demolish her with the chainsaw. I told him to just walk to the back door another way and that if he did chainsaw my rose I'd leave home. It was when he met the fertilizer rep crawling through the Veilchenblau tunnel on his hands and knees that he decided a practical solution other than the chainsaw one should be found. He welded a pipe frame to support the weight of the branches and now we have an inelegant but spacious tunnel. You still have to bend to pass beneath the rose tangle but it's better than crawling. The outer canopy of the tunnel is a mass of powdery purple flowers, and in the tunnel you are enveloped in a sweet musky dusky perfume, I've never smelled myrrh but I imagine myrrh smells like my Veilchenblau on a hot morning.

My lovely reliable Bantry Bay is a cloud of frothy pink draped over the swimming pool fence, and beside her another faithful retainer, Westerland, buds in orange, opens a pale orange, fades to cream and pale pink then strews spent petals over a small brick path between the fence and the pool.

The delphiniums have taken another battering in the wind. There are delphiniums rising from amidst the beds all over the back garden, amongst Penelope and Perle d'Or, the Icebergs and against the orchard fence. They're self-sown and I leave them because I love their blue hues. The week before last they looked like blue spruce forests, sky blue, cornflower blue, inky blue and purple blue, standing tall and straight. This week they are a drunken dishevelled bruised mess. Bloody wind. Delphiniums are resilient though. The stems don't snap. They just fold over and after a day or two the tip of the spike heads for the sun once more. If you pick a stem after the wind and three days of sun it looks like a writhing blue snake. I seldom pick flowers for the house so it doesn't matter much. I feel sorry for cut flowers imprisoned in a vase, shut away from the sun and the rain.

The trees are heavy with leaves. The grass is rampant and the clover has gone berserk; some of the paddocks look as though they have suffered a snow fall, they're thickly sprinkled with white clover flowers. The chimney bees are delirious and Tony Taiaroa's bees are hysterical in their hives out on the farm.

The early December must do's are almost done. It was so cold through October and November that I was very late draining and cleaning the pool. It is always a race to get the pool drained and refilled before the cows and calves come down for marking. The pool takes two days to fill and if the weather is hot and the cows are down they have first call on the water. Even when I'm not filling the pool, cows have first call on the water. It is a salutary reminder of how precious water is and how flower gardens, in times of water shortage, are a very great luxury. A thirsty cow on a hot dry day can drink about forty litres of water. If we have two hundred cows in the paddocks that is a lot of water being prioritized for cows.

The drive has been sprayed with Round Up and the weeds have crinkled into dust. I'm not a great spray user, but gravel drives always sprout weeds and you could lose your mind trying to pull the weeds by hand. The hedges have been trimmed. I would never have hedges by choice. They are unnatural to look at and they require a lot of upkeep, but they have been there since the house was built and they do keep the wind out.

Dear Virginia

Your water calculations are different from mine. I turn on the hose and water the garden without thinking about where the water's come from. My plants have never known anything but chlorinated and fluoridated water. This is why they have no tooth decay. To a townie it is astonishing to hear about the amount of water a cow drinks. I just hadn't thought about it.

I do have to water one animal — the cat. He won't drink tap water. I leave a bucket out for rain water for him and he sips delicately at that.

Dear Janice

There has not been a frost since the last week in November. I learned something from the frosty spell: for the first time since we have been here I covered the strawberries on cold nights. I began the covering using old silage wrap, but it's heavy and stiff to drape about. At the A&P show I discovered a new product called microclima. It is a lightweight plastic fabric which you can use in tunnel culture instead of ordinary plastic sheeting; because it is so light and fluffy I just swished it out over the strawberries every time a frost threatened. The strawberries have ripened earlier than they usually do in a cold spring.

The berries are huge, speckled with bumps, shiny and very sensuous. On a hot day the smell of ripe strawberries rises from the garden. It is intoxicating. Strawberries taste so good when they are warm from the sun. Imagine the taste of a luscious dark red strawberry dripping juice — well, a sun-warm berry picked straight from the bush tastes more fragrant, more pungent than your imagination can conjure. Strawberries should not be served cold from the fridge.

Last night I picked two three-litre bowls of strawberries. We overdosed on strawberries with cream and icing sugar. The bulk of the pick is being processed into strawberry conserve, an elevated sort of jam where the strawberries are preserved whole in syrup. I seal the conserve in hexagonal-shaped jars with gold lids and it makes wonderful Christmas presents. I'm sure there is a formal recipe, but this is how I've always made conserve. It is very simple.

> I let the strawberries stand overnight in an equal weight of sugar. When the sugar has dissolved around the strawberries I put the whole lot in a pot and simmer it very gently for a while.
>
> To determine whether the conserve is ready I take a spoonful of the syrup and put it on a saucer and leave it to cool.
>
> If a skin forms on the cold syrup the conserve is ready. I pour the conserve into sterilized jars and seal it straight away.

Dear Virginia

I just can't believe the amount of strawberries you harvest! I have white alpine strawberries that crop intermittently, not all at once, so you go out and hunt down one or two and eat them in the garden. Your strawberries reminds me of my first paid job — Wainui Beach, strawberry picking in the school holidays and before school. Back-breaking work. Since then I've always hated seeing strawberries against black plastic. I was earning money to go to university.

It's a week later, in another break between rain squalls, and the garden is all knitted together with sweet peas twined round everything. Pink, smelly sweet peas knit a row from Graham Thomas to New Dawn, over old stocks, lychnis, forget-me-nots. How can it be that the translucent, butterfly-delicate sweet pea is the flower that best survives heavy rain? It is also the smelliest plant at midday when lots of plants don't smell. Nicotianas smell most at dusk but it's wonderful to smell the sweet peas as I go about my gardening.

The only place that isn't tangled up in sweet peas is one small orderly bed of Asian red lettuce, boiling and bubbling up from the ground, glossy, red ochre colours, and over it all, one large and now thriving zucchini plant which shades the lettuce. All are getting on amicably.

The back of the garden is now a sea of mauve (catmint and lavender) and white (round hydrangea heads, small campanula trumpets, and huge bishop's flowers which just pop up where they feel like it), with a few yellow Graham Thomases and one tall artichoke. The hostas in pots on the verandah have tall flower-heads the same colour as the nepeta.

On December 16 the first cicadas started carolling!

Dear Janice

This year, like you, I rediscovered globe artichokes. They are a wonderful vegetable to fill the late spring hiatus when there is nothing but tired silverbeet remaindered from winter. The books say that artichokes don't like cold. They also say they do not breed true from seed. When I planted out the plants grown from the same seed packet (Artichoke Green Globe Improved), they were not all the same. Two of the plants shrivelled to ground level and didn't recover after the frosts. Three plants survived and produced a host of wonderful florets which we ate. There are still some left. I am letting them grow large to see if I can duplicate the Isman Bavaldy's artichoke dish I told you about; the one with the asparagus and the sweetbreads, it certainly is not structurally possible with a small artichoke. Did you know that the petals are called bracts? Yes, you probably did, being a wordsmith.

Forget about the Isman Bavaldy; the best way to eat artichokes is the way we ate them as children. Mother dropped them into boiling salted water for about 15 minutes. Eating artichokes was an 'art form'. We began with the butt of the outside bracts; we called these the arty, and proceeded to the soft heart which we called the choke. We dipped everything in butter and ground pepper. Mother was ahead of her time in the cooking department. No one else ate arty chokes.

Another early summer saviour is the broad bean. My plants are chest-high and roped into line against the wind; they are loaded with beans from foot to tip. In an earlier letter I was rude about broad beans being unpalatable and about *Cuisine* magazine chefs making a virtue of unpalatable vegetables. I am actually an avid devourer of *Cuisine* magazine *and* broad beans. When we were children, mothers used to cook broad beans when the beans were mature. They were like grey bean bullets with the thick outer casing split half off. Thanks to an influx of foreign cooking styles, broad beans are now cooked when they are young and tender. I pick them when the pods are slim and the beans are not much bigger than peas nestled in the white furry pod bed. I pick them about ten minutes before they are to be cooked. Broad beans make an interesting warm salad.

Tonight I tipped beans into a pan with a dash of olive oil and quickly tossed them until they were bright green, then I added some chopped spring onions, removed the pan from the heat and poured a little balsamic vinegar over the beans and lastly added some crunchy bacon pieces and ground a whole heap of pepper over the mix. *Voilà*, warm bean salad. You can add croutons at the last minute for a more substantial salad if you want.

Carrot thinnings are wonderful to eat. They are the tiniest sweet pale orange baby carrots, and eating them makes me feel like a carrot murderer. The potatoes have been mounded with earth; I hope they will be ready for Christmas. I have baby beetroot, green peas, sweet corn, broccoli, fennel, cauliflowers, runner beans, mesclun and lettuces all in various stages of development. The first lettuces, Little Gem, are almost finished. The fraudulent tomatoes, purchased already in flower, are forming tiny tomatoes in their pots on the terrace. The Oregon Spring tomatoes I grew from seed are potted out and some are in the flower bed under the grapevine where the days are long and hot, a smidgen of Tuscan sun. I forgot about the courgettes until last week. I rushed to plant zucchini seeds, Zephyr (yellow and green) and Ambassador (dark green), into pots. Already they have burst through the soil, they are fast movers. Under one of the microclima tunnels green peppers grow, and under the other a telegraph cucumber and tons of sweet basil. The tunnels are made of old polythene water-pipe hoops with the plastic stuff over the top.

Of course there are far too many vegetables for us to eat but it is nice to be able to give them away. We have Sam, a Lincoln University student, working here for his practical experience during the holidays. He eats with us Monday to Friday; he will help eat the vegetables. Lincoln students usually prefer Mr Wattie's vegetables but I do not indulge them in this heinous preference very often. I think it is good for them to eat strange vegetables like artichokes and broad beans.

Did you know that Mr Wattie was born in Hawarden? Probably not.

Dear Virginia

Because of the huge canning factory in Gisborne when we were growing up, I assumed Mr Wattie was a Gisborne child, suffering the same schooling as we had. I'm amazed you live near his birthplace. Does it smell of tomato sauce?

I have grown broad beans only once. I love eating them and I love them as things to feel — the furry little cases — and things to smell. But in a too-small garden I don't do broad beans. A couple of nights ago I was at friends' for dinner and they served tiny broad beans from their garden. I think they read *Cuisine* magazine too.

Weeding now is more like arranging hair — I comb through the plants and make them look stylish. The verandah bed is full of bog sage (which always needs trimming), geums, cranesbill geraniums, and viscaria. It's lovely to just fluff the beds up, arrange them. There's no soil in sight.

This might be the last letter till after Christmas. I can't be Superwoman, and shopping, wrapping, placating, negotiating — all those Christmas tasks — will take up most of my time for a while.

Dear Janice

Yes, it is almost Christmas. Next Sunday we go to the Road Party. The Road Party has been held on a Sunday in December every year for the last thirty-eight years. Everyone living or working on the road is invited. This year it is being held at Mt Whitnow at the very end of the Virginia road.

December is time to divide and shift the bearded irises. A friend who knows these things says my irises are not flowering with great enthusiasm because they are in need of a chop and change. Interestingly the old pale blue irises that have flowered in front of the garage forever without any intervention always produce large numbers of stems. The fancy super hybrids are the reluctant bloomers. They are very temperamental. I shall lift them all and chop their rhizomes.

Did you know that irises are named after the Greek Goddess of the Rainbow? Yes, you probably did. Yesterday I cut one stem, a regal stem carrying six flowers of purple and white frilly petals. I put it in a tall blue wine bottle and stood it on the kitchen bench where it towered magnificently to the height of the extractor fan, adding a touch of royalty and elegance to the domestic ordinariness of the room. But you don't like picking flowers, I hear you say. I was saving it from being torn apart by the wind.

The starling I wrote of last time has moved on. The brood has grown and flown the nest. A pair of sparrows has moved in. They are busy building a nest, flying to and fro carrying silver birch twigs, moss and dry grass stalks. A bird's life is a tough life, as I said before. When we demolished the Thuya and removed all the debris I noticed a thrush perched on the fence, a clutch of worms wriggling in its beak. It stood for a long time just looking. Later I saw it hopping about the demolition site searching for its babies.

The poor hapless oystercatchers — this year they built their nest in the Willows paddock. I found the nest quite easily. An oystercatcher's nest is called a scrape. There were two eggs laid in a small depression in the middle of a dried cow pat. The eggs were almost as big as hen's eggs, pale olive green with brown speckles, beautiful eggs. The Willows is a thoroughfare paddock, a foolish place to lay eggs, but they were safe until the cows came in. I took a concrete dog bowl out and every time we shifted a herd of cows through the Willows I covered the scrape. The oystercatchers seemed happy with this arrangement because they would return to sitting on the eggs after we passed. However, one morning I went out and everything had gone, birds, scrape, eggs, the lot. No evidence of what had happened. Did the oystercatchers resent the interference and destroy the eggs? Did a hawk eat them, or a ferret, or did they hatch perchance? Who knows, but it is tough being a bird.

Today the wind is stiff, cold, but the sun is shining. The lawns need mowing again, I must go out and plant another patch of mesclun and another row of peas. Whenever I work in the vegetable garden the pet lambs stand at the fence and watch. Citronella, Persephone and Theresa are all ewe lambs so they will join the ewe flock when they are grown up. Very Annie Mary, the pet calf, stands at the fence, too, looking through the wire circles with doleful eyes.

Whoops, I didn't send this. I was overtaken by the early weaning and dipping, strawberry jam and chocolate making, and now it's Christmas Eve day. The Christmas tree has to be sawn down and decorated, the cake is still to be iced, the beds in the shearers' quarters need to be made up for visitors, the blackcurrant sorbet waits to be frozen, the lawns need mowing, and what happens? Toby wakes up with an inflamed paw. He has a barley grass seed stuck between his toes. I ring Zena at the vet clinic. 'We have five beardies booked for barley grass surgery this morning but Kathy will be able to squeeze Toby in at ten,' she says.

When we arrived at the vet clinic we found Mandy with Toby's cousin Morag. Morag is out to it on the stainless steel operating table having a barley grass seed removed from her ear. Kathy asks me to leave Toby and come back in half an hour. I say to Mandy, 'Why don't we go down to the tea rooms and have a coffee?' but neither of us has any money. We are both in dirty farm clothes and boots. We look stringy and tired. Mandy decides to wait. I go off to see Surrey at the organic vegetable shop. He's digging new potatoes in the garden out the back. He's a kind man. He comes in and makes me a cup of instant coffee.

Toby is coming round when I return to the vet clinic. Kathy gives him a shot of something to wake him up and he leaps off the table and scuttles outside where he pees on everything peeable. We zoom home where, two hours behind schedule, I resume the Christmas rush. Why is Christmas in the middle of the barley grass season? Why isn't it in the middle of the winter?

Dear Virginia

Christmas has come and gone. The only hitch was Bunsen eating nearly all of the edible Christmas presents on Christmas Eve when he'd been left at home, alone. I didn't take him to the vet but, for the last few days, he's produced glittery poos in his garden en suite, which indicates that the silver paper around the Christmas chocolates — boxes of them — isn't digestible. He also looks like a small zeppelin.

At December's end, while other people worry about when their rubbish and recycling boxes and bags will be collected, which is a statutory holiday and which isn't, I empty two compost bins. This has to be done methodically. I clear a space close to the bin and place the bin's lid on the ground. Then I heave the bin up and over and put it in the middle of the garden (the only place where there's enough room for it to stand freely and not crush plants). I look at the mound where the bottomless bin was and see black stuff! Compost! I shovel it up into the lid and scatter it around the garden. Then I replace the bin and fill it with the mountain of weeds and clippings my dead-heading, pruning and untangling has created. I dust blood and bone and lime on top, and pour in a bucket of David's horse manure and water that has stood quietly brewing all winter long. The lid goes back on and I feel tremendous satisfaction: not just because I've fed my overworked soil, but also because those huge piles of weeds and clippings have somehow been pressed into two bins. And I know that by next week the bins will be only ¾ full and I will be able to add more. The incredible shrinking compost is a wonder to me. From soil and a seed comes a huge plant. That plant, stuffed into a bin and rotted down, shrinks to a final volume that isn't much greater than before the plant grew so tall. My garden, the *hortus conclusus*, is indeed self-contained.

With the coming of better weather, and that buoyancy I feel when I know there are 364 shopping days to next Christmas and I have survived, I plant more basil. I want as much basil as we can eat — that's a lot. I plant a row of coriander, and more lettuce. I have lots of lettuces, under the zucchini, but I never feel I have enough of them.

Thank God and organized labour (maybe the same entity) for statutory holidays! On December 31, I saw the first beans, hanging limp, soft and so new-looking. I tied up the tomatoes which are doing OK but are overrun by sweet peas. I fussed over the small basils I've just transplanted from seed trays. I marvelled at the different rate of growth between these tiny plants and the sunflowers which, also new to the garden, are racing skywards.

I have no fruit. Lemons were all picked for Christmas. Plums — there are two on one of the trees, none on the other. Feijoas and tree tomatoes and passionfruit, grape, pears and apples thrive but fruit are a long way off. There is rhubarb. I blessed it with compost today. That will give me fruit in January. Why do I have to provide food for myself? Why do I live like a peasant, here in the middle of Wellington, a short stroll from a huge supermarket?

A neighbour, being helpful, has weed-eaten all the nepeta around my mail shed — 'tidying up,' he said. But the same person gave me the best gift I received during this mad season. Cliff's Kidney potatoes for Christmas and Heathers for New Year. The perfect gift for the woman who has everything but potatoes is potatoes.

Dear Janice

We ate Cliff's Kidneys for Christmas too. They were not really ready; I had to dig three plants of very small potatoes for a dinner to celebrate the return of our city daughter. Fleur arrived home on Christmas Eve with her bicycle and kayak on the roof of the car. She spent Christmas Day with us. On Boxing Day she ran over Goat Pass while we hosted our annual Boxing Day lunch party. The day after Boxing Day she kayaked down the Waimakariri River and in the days after that she did it all again. She spent most of her holiday break training for the Coast to Coast. Sometimes I mountain-biked up the road with her. She was very kind and waited for me to catch her at the top of every hill. While Fleur spent her days in an excess of exercise, Harry and I spent ours at half-speed. We enjoyed being leisurely. In the early morning we shifted sheep and checked the water troughs. The rest of the day we swam in the pool, lay about reading books, drank wine and ate Christmas left-overs. The garden took care of itself.

Henry wants to know what Bunsen got for Christmas. Henry found a squeaky rat under the Christmas tree. Fleur had wrapped it in red paper and written his name on the card. Henry cannot read, but a good nose can smell a rat anywhere. He quickly found his present and tore the paper to shreds and then he 'killed' the rat.

Happy New Year from everyone at Double Tops.

January

Dear Virginia

Happy New Year. May all the people who walk through the uplifted Veilchenblau arch be good friends, neighbours and family, and may you be dressed appropriately to greet them. May you eat strawberries after roast lamb with rosemary.

This is the month when blood-red petals fall from pohutukawa trees, and blush dark across the city pavement or the lawns in the Botanic Gardens. The month when round, starry agapanthus bloom beside the motorway, sprout from retaining walls, and clump in old unruly gardens.

I received a beautifully made hanging basket of flowers for Christmas. I planted the plants in the garden and will use the basket as a bird feeder. I don't like hanging baskets of plants. They use excessive amounts of water and nutrients just to stay hanging there, flowering madly in the air, like a ballerina in a tutu hung from the rafters. If I go away for a summer holiday the cat can migrate to the neighbours'. The hanging baskets, however, will be dead by the time I return.

In your city plot tomatoes are ripening, with lots of beans and zucchini. I am exhausted with all these statutory holidays and gardening. Time to go back to the sedentary life of the office.

Dear Janice

Our leisurely week was over on January 2nd. On January 3rd I crawled out of bed at 4 a.m., grumbling and groaning. I'm a night person and night persons do not like crawling out of bed before the eastern sky has paled; the morning was deep black.

We were on the tops with our dogs before the sun had risen, with me muttering about not being able to see. The coldest hour of the night is the hour before sunrise. I wrapped my coat tight around my shoulders and waited for the sun. The sky reddened to the east and the hills lightened until we could sort the sheep from the bushes. The sun rose over the seaward hills and the tussocks turned gold in the cool fresh air and I vowed I would become a morning person so I could smell the dawn every morning.

After four days the hill sheep were mustered down and we began the weaning draft before shearing. It drizzled the morning of weaning and the draft took three and a half hours. Harry always takes the drafting gate, and Toby, Tan and I keep the sheep moving forwards. We finished the drafting without any shouting. The drafting yards are the scene of many an argument between couples on farms. The paramount rule to remember at all times is this. If there are three ways to do a job, there are two wrong ways and the boss's way. A universal command in the yards is, 'Open that gate over there and put those sheep through into that yard and then bring that other mob through behind them.' You are meant to know, by some mysterious telepathic process, exactly which sheep and which yards are being referred to. If you get the wrong sheep and the wrong yard you are an idiot. If you get it right you feel you should be congratulated on your perspicacity, but of course you never are. After the weaning drafting it took a day for the sheep to dry and then we began dagging and shearing. You will not believe this but all my clever sequencing of lettuces came to grief at shearing — I was between lettuces and had to buy two for shearers' lunches.

Dear Virginia

I will believe the lettuce lull. Sometimes, when guests are due and I go into the garden to pick a lettuce, I feel resentful. Why spoil this perfect circle of lettuces just for a few minutes of munching? But I cut it, let the white milk drip over the soil, bring it in, and turn it into salad.

And of course I believe in the three rules. Offices work in exactly the same way. There are three ways to do a project. Your own way, which is the efficient way. The boss's way — involving mountains of paperwork, timelines, budget reports, allocations (which are charts on which you have to tally your hours spent). Then there is the third way, the client's way. That is always the right way even though it will be inefficient, and involve much 'reporting', meetings, things called 'milestones', and the counting of sheep — when I'm too stressed to sleep.

Dear Janice

Yesterday as inky purple clouds billowed up the valley from the south into a hot midday, a race ensued between the lawn mower and the storm. It was ewe fair day. I had stayed at home to mow the lawns before the rain. I finished just as the rain came belting down in balls of ice. Thunder, hail, lightning, it was a real summer storm and it rained heavily on into the night. My wilting garden has been relieved by the rain. This morning the green parts of the garden are looking fresh and shiny; the flowers are — bedraggled.

The mountains are stunningly 'winteresque', with a covering of snow to below the tree line. If the sky clears and the wind dies there will surely be a frost. But it is midsummer and the mountains under the snow have an accumulation of warmth in the rocks and stones which should melt the snow from the ground up.

(*Days later.*) We were reprieved. The wind turned warm in the late afternoon, the snow slunk away overnight. The next morning the sky was clear and the sun shining.

There are many birds in the garden, bellbirds, fantails, goldfinches, waxeyes, grey warblers, swallows and all the permanent residents, sparrows, blackbirds, thrushes, but no magpies. Their adolescent offspring will return to mock from the tree tops in the autumn.

Dear Virginia

I am so glad you've told me there are still birds in your garden. After all the trampling cattle and lusty rams, and stoats, and rats, I was getting concerned. I noticed your last letter had a Forest and Bird sticker on it. I was going to report you to them if I heard any more bird horror stories.

We have shrieking tuis here. I prefer blackbirds and I love thrushes. Now that I have wires for the roses to climb along, I also have birds on wires — kingfishers, blackbirds, sparrows, finches, starlings. They line up in the morning for our version of inspecting the troops. If I want to see oystercatchers (and I do — I love them) I go to the beach. I never thought of them nesting inland. Why don't they nest in the part of your farm where the bush is regenerating and no cows parade?

Vivid lime-green dill against blue agapanthus is great. I didn't plan it, or plant it. It just happened. Dahlias glow at the side of the house, in the neglected sleep-over bed. And cosmos — oh thank God for cosmos. It fills spaces. It's like the essential party guest. You know they will show up. They will look as though they are enjoying themselves. They won't eat or drink too much. And, best of all, they won't draw attention away from the more important guests. Hydrangea flowers, great bosomy things, are matrons standing along the wall, watching the dance.

Dear Janice

I have the window open to the afternoon and I can hear a pig screaming, screaming, screaming and a pack of dogs yelping with excitement. The ferret trappers are hunting pigs on Mt Mason. I hope the pig dies soon. I hate pig hunting. Someone once described it as base atavism; it is. Now the afternoon has hushed. The pig has surrendered. The hunters will stick the pig's throat and bleed all the blood out. They will gut it and one of the hunters will carry the kill across the creek to the road, the carcass slung over his shoulders, the remnant blood trickling down his neck and soaking his shirt. All that blood and guts and squealing is just heart-wrenching. Meanwhile the birds twitter on unperturbed. Violent death; it happens all the time in the country.

Dear Virginia

No! I still can't bear to know about it. I know I'm being ridiculous. I often saw the results of pig hunts in Gisborne, as a child, and I ate them. It's the city's schizoid attitude to its food supply — we keep ignorant about the cruelty of factory farming, and the blood and guts of hunting. And we keep ordering BLTs, and chicken satay in cafés, and dining on venison for special occasions.

Dear Janice

I'm sorry about the pig letter. Flowers. The midsummer bloomers are beginning their blooming, white shasta daisies, purple cone flowers (*Echinacea*) and the green cone flowers. Shasta daisies are annoying after a time because they fall about in disorderly fashion and smother other plants, but at the moment they look very lovely, like debutantes coming out at their first ball, pristine white, glowing. Late January is the time to cut some of the early perennials back. This will guarantee a flowering in the autumn. The hardest task in perennial gardening is deciding how much to trim in midsummer. You have to make sacrifices to achieve an autumn display. If you cut now, you cut the tail-end flowers off and suddenly the plants are bereft clumps of shorn green. You have to convince yourself of the benefits to come. It's akin to saving, money in the bank for a rainy day. The roses have been dead-headed of their dead heads, spent delphiniums have been chopped to ground level, and the sidalceas and the blue scabiosa have been trimmed.

I will tell you of my favourite stand-bys. You describe yours so colourfully. My blue scabiosa falls into your essential party guest category, a low-growing perennial planted along the edge of many of the borders, it is dotted all summer with pale blue flowers. Larkspur is another stand-by, and sweet william which I planted once, maybe twenty years ago. The sweet williams seed in perpetuity as do the opium poppies and the white pyrethrum daisies. Sweet william is a biennial and does not flower in the first year, a dull guest to begin with.

The opium poppy I would describe as a persistent party visitor, loud, hogging the limelight then turning ugly before the do is over. The poppy seeds germinate everywhere; I pull most of them out, I leave just enough to effect a frothy dark pink display over Christmas. I do not collect the white bud sap for opium smoking, but I do cut the fat poppy heads and dry the seed for cooking.

Another plant I allow to remain for seed harvesting is coriander. The seeds are still green just now, but when they begin to ripen I will cut the seed heads and hang them upside down to dry. It would be more efficient to buy coriander seeds but why submit to the ever insistent drive for efficiency — home-grown tastes better. When I need ground coriander I toast my seeds and grind them with a pestle and mortar.

Dear Virginia

Thanks for that. Somehow chopping and slashing and dead-heading plants doesn't seem violent. Maybe it's just because they don't scream.

Now that the growth explosion has happened, the new paths (that the designer said were too narrow, remember?) are hidden under arching cornflowers, catmint, huge sunflower leaves, and tomato bushes. I do remove the laterals, but somehow lots of tomato flowers appear in all directions and I always end up with a tomato jungle. So, the paths are how I like them, invisible. I bush-wack my way down the garden, knowing exactly where to place my feet on the smooth concrete hidden under pumpkin flowers and creeping mats of thyme.

My artichokes are huge and I might try the mad Alice B Toklas recipe. I have one plant at each corner of the catmint bed. One is called Gertie and another is called Alice. This is brilliant garden design (!) because catmint is kind of frothy and loose and floppy, and to have it contained by four artichoke plants is nice. I've got the four new plants, from David, the friend with the lifestyle block up the coast. He says they grow fine from seed, so we shall see whether your book or David's plants are right. (He's an actuary who gardens rather than a farmer, but, like all financial people, he has a quiet air of authority about him and I believe him utterly about artichokes.).

The passionfruit has taken off after looking like a painting for a year. It's over 6 feet high suddenly and taking over the clothes line.

Now I must have a serious talk with you about Veilchenblau. Mine looks healthy, nice light green leaves. I don't expect it to 'ramp' until it's a bit older because it gets little sun at ground level where it is, in the corner by two fences. BUT — it has not flowered. There were no buds on it at all! Everything else has flowered, blown, and gone. It was 'designed' (by me) to be behind the catmint and flowering with them, the same pink-tinted blue. But this is not happening. I'm green with envy, not chlorophyll, thinking about yours on its new frame. I laughed at the idea of the fertilizer man crawling underneath it, but there was jealousy in with the laugh.

Dear Janice

Late January and the broad beans and all their wonderful little nitrogen-fixing nodules are in the compost heap, the peas have been uprooted. In their place broccoli and purple cauliflowers, late sown Kinbi carrots (Kinbis are golden yellow and sweet) and beetroot are gaining momentum for the winter harvest. The second crop of peas did not come up. After waiting and searching for signs of life I explored the row. Not one pea. It was as if I'd never planted any seeds. Had I had a senior moment? No, that was a silly thought. The peas hadn't rotted because you can always see the evidence of rotted seed, so I concluded that a smart, efficient bird or a rodent had, seed by seed, eaten the lot. Did you know that hungry mice will dig pea seeds? It's too late in the season to sow another row, so no more green peas till next year. The scarlet runner beans on their tepee are very slow. No beans have set. The dwarf purple beans have not set either. Beans like heat.

The Cliff's Kidney potatoes are a pleasure to dig. White oval potatoes roll from the black dirt as the fork prongs lift upwards. The Baby carrots when pulled are bright orange with pea-green tops, I take them straight inside and wash them, chop them, cook them for tea. It would be much easier to call at the supermarket and buy 'ready to go' vegetables in clean plastic bags, but the work is a small price to pay for the home-grown flavour and hey, no plastic bags. The courgettes, which I neglected to plant out until after Christmas, are retarded. I hope that they will make compensatory growth, as livestock does if it has been through a period of deprivation. Under the cloches the basil is bushy and the cucumbers are growing exponentially. We have been eating lots of basil mayonnaise with tomatoes (bought) and new potatoes.

And what to do with an excess of cucumbers? This is a cucumber recipe called tzatziki which is very good.

Tzatziki

1 cup of yoghurt cheese
2 cloves of crushed garlic
½ cucumber peeled, cored and finely chopped
1 tablespoon of fresh mint
salt

Stir all the ingredients together and serve. Tzatziki is a good partner to lamb kebabs.

Yoghurt cheese is strained yoghurt. To make yoghurt cheese: line a sieve with a clean tea towel, place over a basin, pour the yoghurt in and allow it to drain for a few hours. The yoghurt will be thick and creamy.

And the lettuces? After the glitch in lettuce production over the main shearing I now have an oversupply of lettuce, but we are

planning to shear the two-tooths and the wether lambs next week so some of the crop will be consumed. I think I will make a Presbyterian Ladies' ewe fair salad lunch for the shearers. The Presbyterian Ladies' lunch is like the shearers' standard summer lunch only a bit fancier. The lettuce is very finely shredded and it is topped with quartered boiled eggs and quarters of tomato. The potato is creamy mashed. There are two meats, and pickles, and home-made mayonnaise. A journalist once wrote of the Hawarden Presbyterian Ladies' ewe fair lunch in the ewe fair *Press* report. He wrote that there are two sureties in life, taxation and death, and that the aforementioned lunch had joined them as the third. The ewe fair lunch has been the same since we began going to the fair in 1975; old-time diners say the menu hasn't changed in essence since the ladies won the contract to provide meals to the Hawarden Ewe Fair in the 1930s. Do not laugh at the finely shredded lettuce salad. Crisp Iceberg or Great Lakes lettuce salads have been rediscovered. They are a welcome contrast to floppy designer lettuce salads. I find cold meat, pickle and hot smashed potato strangely comforting. They remind me of childhood summer lunches, the beach and freedom.

Dear Virginia

Do you think the next generation will be growing food to eat? Most young people I know have no time for gardening, or for cooking from scratch. Will all this knowledge of nature, and enjoyment of living in and with nature, just disappear? If I thought that those kids' gardening books of mine would turn one child into a gardener, particularly a vegetable grower, I'd be satisfied.

Dear Janice

I don't know if the next generation *will* be growing food to eat because I recently heard vegetable gardening and cooking described as quaint cottage hobbies. That was a shock, to hear that my lifestyle was a hobby. I am sure that your gardening books for children will have grown more than one vegetable gardener!

Midsummer is time to resurrect the trickle pipes. In Kit's memorial garden around the duck pond I have installed a trickle system. Every winter the trickle pipes become overgrown and sink into the long grass and dirt. Of course one never plans ahead. The nor'west winds blow, the sun is hot. When the plants have almost expired in the dry dirt I'm frantically digging and tugging to extricate the black pipe which loses most of its trickle whiskers in the process. If I leave the trickles exposed over winter the hares amuse themselves by biting off all the whisker pipes about an inch from the main pipe. Either way it's hard to win, nature is a wily opponent. This spring I planted more cabbage trees, flaxes, black beech trees, ribbonwoods, golden totoras and kowhai around the pond. Some of the new plants are on the trickle lines and the rest will have to be drench-can watered.

Kit's memorial garden is an exercise in how not to plant a wilderness area. We were desperately sad, not practical, when we conceived the idea. Harry fenced off a triangle of paddock around the back paddock duck pond. We placed the big rock in front of the pond then we asked all our friends to come and help us plant the area. We had no plans. Everyone brought beautiful nursery-grown natives which we planted with great tenderness and enthusiasm. Most of the plants died within the first year from drought, flooding, frost, wind and rabbit browsing. The site is very exposed, boggy in winter, concrete in summer. The only plants to survive that situation were the flax and cabbage trees from the farm swamps and the tussocks from the hills. In year two we planted again. We caged the plants in chicken wire to deter the rabbits. We laid trickle for the summer. That solved the dry problem, but the following winter was wet and some of the plants drowned. We replanted. In year five we had a major drought followed by the severe winter when the farm froze solid. The cold murdered the cabbage trees and the totaras and some of the flaxes. Disasters are never irretrievable; the cabbage trees sprouted from the trunk base, we replanted the totaras and flaxes. We searched for plants which would survive the climate and the dirt; beech on the high ground, South Island kowhai, olerias, broadleaf, ribbonwood, lacebark. Every year the garden grows more leafy, a living memorial to Kit and all his classmates who died with him at Cave Creek.

Dear Virginia

I am sure the trees will continue to grow in Kit's memorial garden, and the sun to flash off the stone. We have no memorial to Boyd in this garden. We weren't gardeners then, thirty years ago, in a house in the East End of London. And this garden was never a part of his life. His place was, and I think still is, the mountains, especially the granite Sierra of California. But I guess my gardening is a way of addressing my loss. I learnt never to waste anything, to treasure fleeting beauty, to dig deep in the soil, to care for living things.

And so it is that every summer evening I weed carefully around the basil seedlings, lettuces and spinach and silverbeet. I pull the spent sweet pea haulms off their sticks and carry them to the compost. I reassemble the composts, adding seaweed from mulching moments on the beach. I take my time, just happy to be outside amongst the leaves, the sun and shadows, wind, birds and insects. I find an Emperor Gum Moth in the garden. The huge wings are bigger than those of sparrows.

Dear Janice

I weed the garden on summer evenings too and sometimes I take the puppies walking which is how I discovered the plight of the Algerian oaks I'd planted down at the cattle yards. A case of neglect, I didn't notice their distress over the January busy time. When you plant new trees on dry sites they always require watering in the first year. I use old drench containers filled with water if there is no trickle system in place. The drench container has a tap which you turn on so the water trickles out very slowly. The trees should be mulched to retain the moisture in the soil. Because the summer has not been acutely dry I didn't think of the poor Algerian oaks. Each tree now has its very own red drench container leaking water into the soil.

Dear Virginia

I've had people staying for 2 weeks and then been away on a work trip. This weekend's been the first I've had a chance to disappear into the garden for a long time. It has taken a while to adjust to being there. Somehow this year the garden has rioted and I've lost the battle. Nicotianas, lychnis, honesty, borage (as well as dock, chickweed, tradescantia, convolvulus) are all fighting for space. The sunflowers are as high as the house, higher than the guttering anyway. Albéric Barbier, the lovely buttery centred white rose that's common around Wellington because it was an early settlers' rose, hangs from the verandah almost to the ground! Very like your Veilchenblau, people have to dodge the deadly shoots to get to the front door. On the pergola in front of the back door hangs François Juranville, growing 6 inches in every direction every day, and aiming to poke many eyes out. The cottage is a townie version of Sleeping Beauty's castle. Instead of having a young prince on a horse to hew a path through the brambles, I shall have to do it myself. I am beginning to think ramblers are not a good choice in so small a garden.

Today, faced with all this rampant growth, I knew I'd have to start slowly. I focused first on the microcosm of a vase, rather than the calamity of the garden. I picked alstroemeria — you just tug them from the ground, instead of cutting them. I added

Souvenir de la Malmaison roses — which I love because they smell, and a few Dublin Bay roses, and some dill. I arranged them in a big vase and placed them on the kitchen bench. That felt better. I could now go and tackle the garden.

I fought my way into a border. First, I was irritated by the tiny snails coiled in the silverbeet, and high in the tree tomato. Then I hated those transparent tiny butterfly things with brown-veined wings, that jump when you touch them. They love the rhubarb. And the apple, so covered with fruit that it looks crippled, is covered with spider webs. All this made me feel angry. I had to pull out beans, and be showered with those jumping bean bugs, pick tomatoes, and cut down the finished shasta daisies before I could relax and know that I will be able to reclaim the garden. It will just take time. By the afternoon I was mowing the tiny lawn, and even oiling the lawn mower and secateurs. It had taken me 3 hours to get to that state of happy tinkering, but I was at last there.

You start doing something in the garden, slowly, perhaps reluctantly, especially if you have been crumpled at the office all week, then you gradually become more part of the garden. You become gentler with the plants. You forget all the 'must do' lists from work.

'As your hands work, the world retreats,' to quote Michael Pollan.

Dear Janice

I laughed at your anger at the snails and bugs and spiders. 'I hear what you are saying,' a counsellor might say. She might say that you are really angry with yourself for neglecting the garden but you are taking it out on the snails. Before busy times on the farm I have a gardening blitz. I weed and prune and trim and mow, the garden looks as tidy as a freshly dusted house. I turn my back and two weeks later the garden looks like a teenager's bedroom and I feel like yelling at it. I don't know where to begin to restore order. I like some order, maybe I'm a control freak because I know I couldn't allow roses to ramble the way you do. Veilchenblau is my only rambler and New Dawn is a vigorous climber and they both try my patience. No more time to write, I have to go out into my garden to restore order. I will 'work my hands so the world retreats'.

Dear Virginia

Today I made a major decision. I will not buy any more roses! Roses are too dangerous for a small garden.

A fortnight ago I got a thorn in my calf. I tried to get it out. It stayed put. I bathed it, disinfected it, forgot it. Occasionally during the next few days I would touch the place the thorn had speared me. The pain was like an electric shock. But other than that, I forgot it. After a week my leg was much bigger than the other one. A sore had developed that didn't heal. I went to the chemist. 'No,' he said. 'You must go to the doctor, immediately.' I cancelled two meetings at work and went to the doctor's. He said he couldn't remove it until the infection was under control. I feasted on antibiotics for two days then returned to the doctor's. Instruments were laid out. A nurse swabbed the wound with something that numbed the area. She removed the crust that had formed over the angry crater. Another doctor was consulted. Then the two doctors and the nurse backed out of the room and told me I had to wait 5 minutes before they would return to try to extract the thorn. I waited. I was bored. I examined the instruments lined up on a tray beside the bed. With one, a sharp little box-cutter-thing, I poked around in the sore. A thorn, the shape of a sail, was lying near the surface. I picked it up with some tweezers and looked at it closely. The medical team returned and I showed them the thorn. 'I've done your work for you,' I said. They told me to keep taking the antibiotics.

I recovered. The leg healed. Before work yesterday I hung one of my best silk shirts on a hanger under the verandah to dry, after hand-washing it. I didn't want it out in the full sun and wind. When I came home the shirt was impaled on a nearby Albéric Barbier rambler. After I'd untangled it there were so many pulled threads in the shirt I knew it had done its last PowerPoint presentation. Damn!

So today, from my deck chair, I look at the tentacles of Albéric Barbier, growing a foot a day in every direction, covered in sail-shaped prickles, and I make the decision. In future I will have grapevines and wisteria up the pillars and under the verandah roof. I will get rid of the roses.

February

Dear Janice

Do something about that dangerous jungle of Albéric Barbier! If there weren't a Cook Strait between us I would send John to hew a path to your door. He would make a good knight in shining armour. He would massacre old Albéric Barbier with his hedge trimmer. There may not be much of Albéric left, but you would be set free.

The February winds blow laced with thistle down and flaking silver-birch catkins. Like sand in a desert storm the papery seeds of the birch trees penetrate every crevice, every orifice in the house. They even find their way through shut windows, strew the carpets, float in the teapot. The wee flakes fill the roof gutterings and lie on the surface of the swimming pool where they absorb the water and sink. The seeds add hours of work to pool maintenance but I persuade myself the birch tree is worth the inconvenience, especially the Swedish cut-leaf birch, *Betula pendula*. This birch is a slender, graceful tree with serrated leaves. It grows tall with a paper-white trunk. Pendula is the earliest birch in leaf and already its summer is over. The leaves have yellowed and will soon drop — into the swimming pool!

In February the surface of the pool is littered with dead bumble bees. They are fatally attracted to the blue water. The whole garden crawls with bumble bees. They love blue flowers and seethe over the lavenders, catmint and the scabiosa. The artichokes we didn't eat grew into flowers, great orbs of purple bristles with a strange texture like a plastic hairbrush. In one large bloom I counted fifteen crawling bees searching for pollen, for nectar, or maybe just a blue-purple fix? I know nothing of the life of a bumble bee, where it lives, how it winters over, do you? I rescue the bees if I see them clinging to flotsam in the pool; if they don't find a life raft they float on their backs on the clear water until they drown. I have to swim fast on bumble bee days in case the bees mistake me for a life raft. Bees cling and sting. Kingfishers like the pool too; one flew down and sat on the deck railing yesterday. I suspect he was checking for fish. He ate a chlorinated moth, which cannot have been to his liking because he spent a long time trying to 'hoik' it out.

It seldom rains in February. The flowering plants are falling over half-spent. The blooms bleach in the dry sun. There is wind, dry wind which sucks out more moisture than hosing can replace. I must water the garden every day. The poplars have panicked. Some are turning yellow and shedding their leaves as a precautionary measure. The driveway has sprouted a wonderful field of wheat in the heat. The shingle truck must have carried a bulk wheat load before it carried our Christmas shingle.

Whenever Harry is away, water is my biggest nightmare. We have our own farm water scheme: the water is pumped from a gallery well beneath the North Waipara River to two tanks on top of a small hill. The water is reticulated around the paddocks from these tanks. My biggest dread, ever since it once happened to me, is that all the water will run away. Cattle are serial water thieves. They love playing with troughs and ballcocks, especially in the summer when they drill for water, digging up pipes and breaking the pipe connections and making fountains. Cows love drinking from cold water fountains. It's fun and refreshing and they cool their hot feet at the same time. If the burst pipe is not noticed, all the water in the system drains away. There is a reserve tank to switch to, but if the whereabouts of the hole is a mystery you cannot switch over until the leak is found. The cows become very thirsty and angry, like drinkers at a pub with no beer. The pump sometimes breaks down. The system can become airlocked. It's all a horrible nightmare when you don't understand pumps and pipes and airlocks. Harry carries a map of the water system in his head. There is no paper map so it is difficult for anyone else to work out where the pipes lie. Harry says it is perfectly logical. I disagree. I say it is as logical as my kitchen cupboards where he cannot find anything.

Dear Virginia

My garden is dry in February too. Dead sweet pea vine lies in a pile on the deck, like an old fishing net. I rub my hand through sages and smell the ripeness, feel the stickiness. I like to do this after I've brought in the sun-stiff washing. My garden watering problems are limited to a leaky hose/tap join, but I solved that by buying a new one. I wish I had a system for gathering all the rain water from the roof to use on the garden but the Wellington City Council insists that storm water goes down the drain.

Instead of cows playing with water I have Bunsen — a small cow in size — who loves turning round and round in his paddling pool, trying to dig the pool deeper. We call him the hairy hippopotamus.

I've repotted never-die red geraniums in terracotta pots for the winter. I use terracotta pots in winter, when there's plenty of rain, and plastic pots in the summer. With plants that like dry feet, like geraniums, you need as much drainage and evaporation as you can get. In the summer the terracotta dries out too quickly and all the nutrients in the soil are leached out with the necessary watering. Instead of your old drench containers for slow and steady watering, I add a large paua in the top of each pot, on the surface of the soil. After I water, I fill the paua shell. The trickle-down effect begins, through the paua shell holes. It keeps the pot moister for longer. When there's no water in the shell, a quick refill and the plant's fine for another while.

Catmint makes a mauve haze at the garden's end, from which comes the hum of bees. Catmint: my very own bee-loud glade. What do I know about bees? Very little that makes any sense to a project manager. In one bee's honey-gathering life, he will fly about 800 kilometres and make approx 1 teaspoon of honey. Every day a bee makes only enough honey to coat a pinhead. I think about the bee's working life when I'm in the office, gazing out the window at the blue sky. I'm not sure which one of us has the better employment contract.

This month it's shasta daisies and catmint, and those good old cosmos, that keep the garden flowering. There are red bean flowers, and a few yellow tomatoes. There are the wonderful soft protective paws of zucchini flowers. There's bergamot. And a few roses, of course — Graham T, Sparrieshoop, Caroline, Lady Hillingdon and Dublin Bay. The others are all oncers. (Yes, I changed my mind. I haven't got rid of the roses. How could I?) But best of all there are the lilies. I don't remember planting them but I must have, each side of the rosemary path. They look as though they have drilled themselves out of the ground, tall, pointed cones of green. I wait impatiently. I wish I could check their job descriptions and project timelines on an Excel spreadsheet to see when they'll deliver — flower, that is. Maybe I'm getting institutionalized.

Dear Janice

A February garden in the Hawarden hills is a dilapidated garden. Like the July garden the plants are in limbo, regrouping for the change of season. They await the autumn rains and dews to gather strength and flower again before the winter. The catmint, scabiosa and pink daisies I trimmed in mid-January are just beginning a second flowering. The lovely shastas, the summer debutantes, have fallen in drunken disarray, fading and browning. Their ball is over. They are almost ready to be cut back. The lychnis, the pyrethrum daisies, and the bergamot have been executed, and barrow-loads of desiccated flower-heads carted away. The lavenders should be trimmed. Why can't shrubs be sprayed with a fixative when they reach the optimum size and shape?

I know you have been on many musters over this year of garden letters and that you are probably tired of mustering by now, but I have to take you on one more because it falls into the 'strange but true' category. Last week we mustered the ewes off Mt Lance. Mt Lance is a rough native block with scrubby gullies, patches of beech and steep rocky outcrops. We were mustering the ewes down towards the gate into Tricky Spur and after four hours we were almost there. The sun had disappeared behind the hills. I was standing on the bottom track when out of the sunset I saw sheep curving around an outcrop high above me. I knew that the sheep had overshot the gate and that if I didn't do something very quickly the whole mob would stream back from where they had come. I whistled Toby up the hill. I lost sight of him in the gloom — he looks like a matagouri bush at the best of times. I radioed Harry on my little handheld RT to say we had a crisis and then I resumed whistling and hoping. I saw the sheep stop and stare and then my radio rang. I pressed the talk button and Harry said, 'I've arrived to find a Blue Beardie here, but he doesn't know what to do next. Do you want to tell him what to do ?' 'Yes,' I said, 'put Toby on.' Harry put the RT to Toby's ear and I called, 'Come out, Toby, come out.' A few seconds later the sheep moved off with Toby barking behind them. Harry told me later that he put the RT to Toby's ear, Toby listened to what I had to say, then took off. Modern technology, eh!

Dear Virginia

For next Christmas I would like a walkie-talkie RT so I can direct Bunsen to his en suite lawn and shout at him when he decides to relieve himself in what he thinks of as the upmarket lavender loo instead, where toileting comes with an aromatic tummy tickle.

Vegies are not so good this year. There are lettuces and silverbeet. Tomatoes — a few. Beans — not heaps. Zooks (about 6 in total), and herbs — parsley, basil, thyme, chives, mint. See — it isn't always perfect! There are ripe grapes on the garage but not enough to fill a bath tub. The rhubarb is covered with little moth things — horrid because there are so many of them. They cover me when I go near the rhubarb. They are sap suckers. The rhubarb looks wan, and sucked. Like yours, my plants are in limbo right now. I will lie in a deck chair and continue reading William Morris on gardens.

Oh, the advantage of living within walking distance of a great public library. Thank you, Wellington City Council. Plant simple flowers, Morris said, not over-hybridized ones that can't be fertilized, are too heavy for their stalks to support, scream their colours at you, and generally look ridiculous. I agree with him.

'Be shy of double flowers. Choose the old columbine where the clustering doves are unmistakable and distinct, not the double ones where they run into tatters.' Are your columbines clustering doves? He noticed single flowers attract bees and butterflies more. I see this is true when I watch the bees working in my garden. Scoop a few bees out of your pool and ask them which they prefer, single or double.

We have such variety of food in our gardens now. Globalization has been good for food growers. More than Morris had, and much more variety than the gardeners of medieval England that I've also been reading about. Tomatoes were brought to Europe from South America in the 16th C. Potatoes, which had been cultivated by Peruvians since 750BC, were brought from Peru by Sir Francis Drake in 1585. Carrot arrived in England from Europe in the time of Elizabeth I. It's incredible to imagine not having these staples today.

Here is a recipe for a vegetable stew English monks used to eat. I dare you to serve it up for shearers' lunches.

Sauce Verte

Blend all together:

2 tbspn chopped mint

1 tbspn chopped parsley

1 tbspn chopped hyssop

1 garlic clove
1 cupful of cider vinegar
50 grams soft breadcrumbs

Mix all together. Add more vinegar if too thick.

What grows fast and loose in your garden now? Here, rose canes are suddenly stretching out, 6 inches, a foot a day. ('Go the Canes' means something rather different in this garden from what it means in the stadium, a few minutes' walk down the road.) While we look skywards at the rose tentacles over pergolas, roofs and gutters, we forget at our peril to imprison the pumpkins. I never buy pumpkin plants. They just arrive, move in with all their family, and take over. This year I built cages round the two most vigorous ones, large cages, each one using 5 metres of chicken wire. By now the chicken wire is invisible, covered by leaves, 50 cm across. Large pumpkins, as yet unweighable, hang from slender, hairy stems. How is it the stem bears the weight? How can so much mass grow from one seed? If you are the Chief Financial Officer of your garden, then a pumpkin gives the best bang for your buck (no contest, being as even the seed is free). By February I've given up pushing the stems back through the wire mesh. It's pitiful to see the leaves, all shriveled up and so determined, pushing through those small holes. But some of them manage, and spread out huge outside the wire. Even yellow, scrunched-up, flowers make it through the holes. If I bend down and part the curtain of leaves I can see the grey dangling pumpkins. I also have one on a climbing bean frame.

They like warmth. They like rich soil. They like water. The pumpkins get blossom-end rot if they dry out and then get a dose of water. A regular supply is what they like. What I will do tomorrow is carry armfuls of the crackly dry sweet pea haulms over to the cages and drop them in so that, when the inevitable catastrophe happens and a pumpkin drops, it will have a soft landing.

Dear Janice

I received your letter this morning. What grows fast and loose in my garden now, fast and loose like your pumpkins and raspberry canes? This foothills climate does not engender a fast and loose attitude in the plants. They're rather more prone to Scottish parsimony in the autumn air. I have plants that ramp, but not in the luxuriant decadent profligacy that your warm garden has, except maybe my Albany Surprise grape. The other plants that overreach themselves, though in a restrained overreaching, are members of the daisy family, Jacob's Ladder, strangulating ground creepers and New Zealand spinach. Do you know New Zealand spinach? It is a rampant rambler in the vegetable garden, its ramblings curtailed only by frost. Once introduced it returns every year and would take over your entire vegetable garden if you let it. It is a useful spinach for Greek spanakopitas and for spinach roulades. You cannot use the stalks, but the leaves are sweet and green.

As for Sauce Verte, it sounds disgusting. No wonder our culinary heritage is so bad, with recipes like that; poor monks. I have a mind to try making the sauce all the same. It might be delicious, *Cuisine* may discover it, chefs will exclaim over the 'mmm, mmmm' subtle combination of vinegar and breadcrumbs. I do not have hyssop. Would it matter?

Dear Virginia

OK. So you wouldn't have been a cook urging medieval monks to eat up all their greens. I haven't tried the recipe either. It's just one of those silly things you come across in a pile of library books on a leisurely Sunday afternoon in the deck chair.

I have given the clothes line over to the passionfruit vine. Since December it's been creeping its way along the parallel plastic lines, tying a tendril round to secure itself every so often. I find a way of hanging the sheets under the line, with just the pegs taking up line space between the leaves. Under the lines the greenish blue globes hang, deserving the sun more than any washing ever could.

I gave Fleur the one large hanging pear today. If I hadn't picked it, I think the branch might have broken. The pear was perfectly ripe. Apples hang all over the 'weeping' apple tree, each fruit helping the tree weep some more. Tree tomatoes hang more lightly. They haven't started swelling yet. Their fruit look like missiles about to plunge to Earth.

Nephews and nieces have visited with their children. I showed them how to slip the tissue-papery covers from the discs on honesty plants and reveal the silver mirrors inside. The kids then pulled the plant out and arranged the silver discs on their bare stems inside in a vase. In winter they'll remind me of that day in February we all stood in the hot, cicada-filled garden.

Or do this: let honesty self-seed in a large patch, 20 or 30 plants. In February, when the seed heads are all dry, on the night of a full moon, invite 20 or 30 friends over in the late afternoon. Give them glasses of white wine and take each person to a plant. Their job is to rub those chardonnay-coloured outer disks off, scattering black seeds underfoot, and baring the so-delicate papery silver discs. Then eat, lots of food — no Sauce Verte — drink some more wine, and wait for the moon to rise. Be wowed by the thousands of silver discs in the moonlight. This is a city activity. In your far distant hills you have the stars to look at.

It's been a good month. The outside world fizzes and pops with the sound of the cicada male-voice choir stridulating. The cat plays with cicadas in his mouth. Bunsen lies in the sun after walks. Bees scumble in the mauve carpet of an artichoke flower. The inside world fizzes and pops, too, with champagne.

Dear Janice

I have a dream. I dream of the city and no mud, of clean clothes and smooth hair, of cafés and films, and the theatre, and lattes — and then I have a day like yesterday. Harry was away at a pest destruction meeting. My dogs and I mustered the ewes from South Mjølfjell to the Double Tops block, and as I stood on a rocky outcrop at the high point of the block I saw the wind in the warm nor'west sky, the bare blue mountains and a wheeling hawk, clouds of dancing insects and floating filaments of spiders' webs with no beginning and no end, and I thought, how could I ever leave my beautiful real world for the city? The city is just tinsel. It's late, eleven o'clock, the night is still and all the stars are out. There could be a frost.

Dear Virginia

I hate to say it but — it's March tomorrow. We've been round the Monopoly board. I'm so glad we started writing to each other. When we met, after not seeing or hearing of each other since school, at the class reunion you and Gillian organized for us all after Kit died, I knew that we'd grown to be two women with totally different lives, but a shared love of gardening and the outdoors.

Do we start this letter writing all over again? I know we will. Maybe we could write for another year, with Gillian this time. She has a coastal garden of native plants at Wainui Beach.

It isn't just the plants that put down roots in our gardens. Every moment we garden, we put down roots too. We belong more. So roll on, another year, another circuit of the Monopoly board.

Dear Janice

You began with Albéric Barbier smothering your house like a Sleeping Beauty castle. I began with the magpies. The magpies have returned with their knowing quardle oodle ardling in the trees. It is timely, I think, to reflect on the future of my farm garden.

In my introductory garden letter, written to you on March 1st last year, I wrote of the bones of the garden, the skeleton on which the garden is fleshed out, the trees, paths and hedges, and I wrote of the hills, gullies, forests and swamps on the farm. They are the foundations. The rest is disposable. Farmers and gardeners come and they go. The gardens are loved and then unloved, dependent on the disposition and the intent of the farmers who own the land. Farms are swallowed in amalgamations. They are sold to investors who don't live on the land. The farm houses are let, the gardens forgotten. The forgotten gardens grow unkempt. In the shrubberies the strong ugly plants strangle the shy graceful plants. The flower borders grow wild. But if the trees are beautiful it does not matter because a legacy has been left. In time another gardener will restore the faded beauty.

I like to think we have left a small tree legacy in the garden and on the farm. One day we will leave the farm and I must accept that my garden may become an abandoned garden. I must not lament this fate. I must accept that my garden is only for me, for now, and not for tomorrow, that when I walk out the gate for the last time I must never look back. I will not grieve for I know that the trees will endure; the eucalyptus trees, the weeping elm, and the copper beech, the silver birches, scarlet oaks, hollies and the claret ashes will shelter and shade the garden. Kit's memorial rock will catch the sun in the mornings and the moon at night. Out on the farm the poplar and eucalyptus shelter belts will lean away from the nor'west wind and in the swamp lands where flax and cabbage trees have grown for hundreds of years the frogs may sing again. I hope the next owners of Double Tops will love this land. What do you hope for your rose-smothered garden?

Dear Virginia

I hope the Wellington City Council will honour their promise to not allow in-fill housing here. I hope the next owners of my cottage garden, my precious garden with its 6-feet-deep soils, sheltered hot spots, and the pealing of the bells rolling off the hill on Sunday mornings — I hope it will be cared for by people who don't concrete it over and turn it into a parking lot.

A parking lot would be a good easy money-earner in this area in the middle of the city. In the '60s I marched at People's Park in Berkeley, California where the University of California, under its regent, Ronald Reagan, decided to turn a park into a parking lot. (Joni Mitchell memorialized it, of course.) We lived the battle for days. The town was under curfew. National Guards patrolled the street. Several people were shot and died. And now, if I leave here, which I will one day do, I will feel a failure if another piece of loved and productive land, productive of food, flowers, relaxation and relationship with the earth, becomes the earth's straitjacket, a pad under a car.

I hope this place does become an old neglected garden when I leave it, a secret garden that one day a child could find by unlocking the garden gate. They might walk through and pick some wild grapes.

Kings Seed Catalogue
Cabbage tree
Silverbeet
Tatsoi   Nepeta
Mico tree   Veilchenblau rose?
Rocket   Feijoas
Silver fern   Tree tomato
Matagouri   Honesty

Do McLachlans
do field burning

Break

Fossick

...ge Trees   astroemeria
...in

...?)

239

...ruary

Dear Virginia

I hope the Wellington City Council will honour their promise to not allow in-fill housing here. I hope the next owners of my cottage garden, my precious garden with its 6-feet-deep soils, sheltered hot spots, and the pealing of the bells rolling off the hill on Sunday mornings — I hope it will be cared for by people who don't concrete it over and turn it into a parking lot.

A parking lot would be a good easy money-earner in this area in the middle of the city. In the '60s I marched at People's Park in Berkeley, California where the University of California, under its regent, Ronald Reagan, decided to turn a park into a parking lot. (Joni Mitchell memorialized it, of course.) We lived the battle for days. The town was under curfew. National Guards patrolled the street. Several people were shot and died. And now, if I leave here, which I will one day do, I will feel a failure if another piece of loved and productive land, productive of food, flowers, relaxation and relationship with the earth, becomes the earth's straitjacket, a pad under a car.

I hope this place does become an old neglected garden when I leave it, a secret garden that one day a child could find by unlocking the garden gate. They might walk through and pick some wild grapes.

Kings Seed Catalogue

Cabbage tree

Silverbeet

Tatsoi

Miro tree

Rocket

Silver fern

Matagouri

Dr McLachlans
do field burning

Break

Fossick

Nepeta

Veilchenblau rose?

FEIJOAS

Tree tomato

Honesty

Borage trees

Campion

Frog

Pukeko (duck?)

Convulvulus

astroemeria